THE
THINGS
THAT
MATTER
MOST

Also by Cal Thomas

Uncommon Sense

The Death of Ethics in America

Occupied Territory

Liberals for Lunch

Book Burning

Public Persons—Private Lives

A Freedom Dream

THE THINGS THAT MATTER MOST

Cal Thomas

HarperCollins*Publishers*
Zondervan

Grateful acknowledgment is made for permission to use excerpts from articles written by the following: Paul Johnson; William Kristol and Jay Lefkowitz; Peggy Noonan; Michael Novak; and Robert L. Woodson, Sr.

Grateful acknowledgment is also made for use of the following excerpts:

"Burt, Loni and Our Way of Life" by Barbara Ehrenreich. Copyright © 1993 by Time Inc. Reprinted by permission.
"Science Without God" by Phillip E. Johnson. Copyright © 1993 by Dow Jones & Company, Inc. Reprinted by permission.

HarperCollins books may be purchased for educational, business, or sales promotional use. For information please write: Special Markets Department, HarperCollins Publishers, Inc., 10 East 53rd Street, New York, NY 10022.

FIRST EDITION

Designed by Nancy Singer

Library of Congress Cataloging-in-Publication Data

Thomas, Cal.
  The things that matter most / by Cal Thomas.
    p. cm.
  ISBN 0-06-017083-2
  1. United States—Social conditions—1980– . 2. United States—Social conditions—1960–1980. 3. United States—Moral conditions.
  I. Title.
  HN59.2.T5 1994
  306'.0973—dc20   93-46041

94 95 96 97 98 ❖/RRD 10 9 8 7 6 5 4 3 2 1

To my grandchildren—Crystal, Timothy, Christopher, Jennifer, Jonathan, and my namesake, Calvin.
To you falls the task of reclaiming the landscape which two generations have let spoil. Your task won't be easy, but the effort must be made.

Acknowledgments

This book would not have been written without the encouragement, support, and example of Dr. Spencer Johnson, coauthor of *The One Minute Manager* and author of *Yes or No* and many other books.

The Things That Matter Most was conceived in Spencer's "writing studio" on the North Shore of the Hawaiian Island of Oahu. If you can't get inspiration there, you can't get it anywhere.

It was Spencer who introduced me to the best agent I've ever had, Margret McBride of the McBride Literary Agency in San Diego. Margret, you are a pro as well as a friend. Thanks for all you have done for me and will do in the future!

I am also indebted to Dr. Robert Norris, who unwittingly gave me the title for this book in a sermon he preached at Fourth Presbyterian Church in Bethesda, Maryland.

Michael Gerson, my researcher and a speech writer for Jack Kemp, is a man who loves libraries, ideas, and facts that others ignore or forget. Mike has become as essential to me as my computer.

Thanks, also, to HarperCollins Executive Editor Rick Horgan, who offered me—after seven other books—my first opportunity with a major New York publisher. You realize, Rick, that if this book sells well, you'll be called "brilliant" and "visionary." We won't consider the alternative.

And to my wife, Ray—this sure beats subways in New York at two in the morning, and cream cheese and walnut sandwiches on whole-wheat raisin bread at Chock Full o' Nuts because we couldn't afford anything else, doesn't it? Thanks for believing in me and for not giving up during the ascent.

Contents

Foreword

by Rush Limbaugh

It is difficult to get a discussion going about the things that matter most in life today. The major media and cultural hall monitors have taken to ridiculing anyone who dares challenge the "accepted" (by them) political, economic, social, or antireligious orthodoxies.

Still, most Americans have more common sense than the political and cultural leadership give them credit for, and when someone articulates their views, they reward that person with their support, loyalty, and enthusiastic approval.

There is no secret behind the growth of my radio and television programs or the bestselling performances of my books. I am simply articulating what many people believe in their heads and hearts, ideas that they so rarely find in the popular media.

This is precisely what Cal Thomas is doing in print and why his syndicated newspaper column has become the fastest-growing political column in the country. It is also why some editors report that Cal gets more mail, pro and con, than all of their other columnists combined.

I must say that I'm not surprised. Cal and I are simply giving huge numbers of people a voice in determining the direction of their country—a voice they've largely been denied for the last thirty years. Decent, God-fearing, hard-working, intelligent, patriotic Americans have suffered a virtual media blackout when it comes to their views and values. Rather than acknowledge their errors and seek to redress the grievances of most Americans, the major media have engaged in ridicule, put-downs, and even censorship.

Like me (!), Cal Thomas has not been put off by such a response. It has caused us to work harder to overcome. We HAVE overcome.

A man of bearing and depth, Cal Thomas writes with a passion born of confidence and the relentless pursuit of truth.

I am indeed fortunate to count Cal as one of my friends. I knew him long before he ever heard of me and he, along with many others, has done much to help me understand and expand upon my natural conservative instincts. Call him a mentor. His ability to think as an individual, coupled with his courage to articulate and promote his convictions, qualifies him as an excellent role model for anyone who seriously longs for truth and high ideals. He will make you think, which is an incredible gift. Far from preaching to the choir, Cal Thomas challenges those mired in conventional wisdom to honestly assess their surroundings and seek substantive, positive change. The man is winning converts.

He is qualified to unmask sham, whether it be the Clinton administration's claim that it represents a generation of "new Democrats," the cultural phoniness of the entertainment industry, the misspending of taxes on programs that don't work, the abysmal failure of "alternative lifestyles" that have brought misery to millions, or so-called "free expression," which has censored all but the corrupt, the cruel, and the base.

Don't just read Cal Thomas. Absorb him. You will be profoundly enthused.

—Rush Limbaugh
New York City

Introduction

Some years I travel more than a hundred thousand miles. It is an antidote to inside-the-beltway fever, a disease that affects almost anyone who spends most of his time as a prisoner of Washington, D.C.

The fever first attacks that part of the brain that leads to rational judgments based not on reality, but on perception. Left untreated, the victim loses all contact with objective truth and begins to assume that he, and those who think like he does in Washington, possess the only truth and that no one else knows much, or what is best for them.

Learning what real people think—as distinct from political junkies in Washington—and then articulating those beliefs is crucial in politics and in punditry.

Understanding this dynamic was central to the rise of Ross Perot in the 1992 presidential race. Perot was seen by many to be a man of the average people and a prisoner of no special interest. Those people gave him more of their votes than any independent presidential candidate has received in history. Perot spoke for many disaffected Americans who feel their government has lost touch with their concerns. Had his ego (and a few nutty ideas) not gotten in the way, Perot might have been president.

People want government to serve them, not the reverse. They want government to represent and preserve their values, not oppose them. Perot understood this, to a point. At a minimum, he gave many a vehicle for venting their anger against a system they believe has failed us.

This is a book for those kinds of people—though not only for followers of Perot. You know who you are. You are people who the "experts" ignore, whose faith and values are regularly criticized and satirized. You are often forced to suffer indignities in relative silence because your access to the major media organs is blocked. You are called names when you refuse to accept the elite's view of the world by people who label you "intolerant" if you question their ideas and practices.

You love your country, but are saddened by the direction in which it is going. You believe patriotism is not conditional. You don't pick and choose which laws to obey or which wars to fight. You are an American, with no hyphens. You believe the motto of America, "Out of many, one," is being turned through class warfare into "Out of one, many," and you fear what this polarization, this balkanization, is doing to your country.

You are people who already know what you believe, and why, and you are not looking for new solutions to old problems. You know that the old solutions work and that by their having been ignored the old problems have returned, bringing some new ones along with them.

You go to church on Sunday (or synagogue on Saturday), where you worship an Authority higher than the state or your erogenous zones. You are frustrated that your faith, values, and beliefs seem to be reflected only in your bathroom mirror.

This is a book for those who feel like aliens in their own land, for those who believed the false promises of the past because they sounded good, but who've come to realize they didn't work and have enough integrity to be willing to try a way that will. Most of all, this is a book for those people who are hungry for facts, and opinions based on them.

There is a growing awareness that government has become

"dysfunctional" and is in need of repair. This feeling is not limited to the "usual suspects" or familiar political and special interest groups. It is surfacing in new places and it offers potential for real change, not the phony change offered by President Clinton, which is really no change at all, but only more of the same.

Taxpayers are tired of being asked to cough up more money for a bigger government that doesn't work and rarely addresses their concerns. Americans now work nearly half the year to support government at all levels, and still President Clinton says many of us aren't paying enough. Hardworking, overtaxed Americans have looked at ever-growing government and its promises, and they are not pleased with the results. They are aware, as perhaps never before, that something has gone dreadfully wrong in the last three decades, and they may at last be ready, under the right leadership, to launch a second American revolution aimed at taking their country back and again creating a government of the people, by the people, and for the people—not government in spite of the people.

While the intentions of those who promised a better world through government were noble, the results were anything but. It is no great sin to make mistakes. It is one enormous sin to perpetuate them by failing to acknowledge that wrong and harmful decisions were made based on a flawed philosophy and falling into denial, refusing to make a course correction.

This is a book that recalls the sixties generation's failed promises and how many now leading the country and culture who are from that generation continue to try to implement the philosophy upon which they were based, in spite of the evidence of failure and misery those broken promises created.

It is about the growing number of voices demanding for themselves and their country a reconsideration of the values in which their parents and grandparents believed.

In the classic parable of the prodigal son, the moment of redemption comes when the young man who has squandered his inheritance on a life of big spending and low living "comes to his senses." America is now at that point. Will she see that the broken promises of the past have not, cannot, and will not work and that another way must be sought, or will she continue hoping against hope and believing against reality and the facts that we can continue as we have and that somehow, someway, we can pull ourselves out of the hog pen?

This is the ultimate question, for individuals and for our nation. What is required is for each of us to focus not so much on parties and platforms, and not on the agenda set by the cultural, media, and academic elites, but on the things that matter most.

In our heart of hearts we all know what they are.

Prelude:
"Don't Stop Thinking About Tomorrow"

The Fleetwood Mac song that became the anthem of the 1992 presidential campaign for Bill Clinton and Al Gore says a lot about the generation that came of age in the sixties.

It is tempting to speculate that the reason they don't want us to stop thinking about tomorrow is so we won't focus on the mess they're making of today. Yet today cannot be divorced from yesterday when, to recall another song, "all our troubles seemed so far away." The past *is* prologue, and if we will not learn from history, we are doomed to repeat it.

What we are as a country is determined in large measure by the way we were in the last generation. What we become will be determined by the choices we make now, in this generation. Bill Clinton ran on a campaign theme of "change," but many of his generation *haven't* changed, and that's the problem. They still cling to ideas forged three decades ago as if they're a life raft. They grew up physically, but many remain the children they were in the sixties, always learning, but never able to come to a knowledge of the truth.

If you slept, Rip Van Winkle–like, through the sixties, you awakened to a different America. The sixties—so celebrated on cable TV and in golden oldie music—was the pivotal point of the recent past: an authentic decade of decision, which unwound the fabric of a culture.

It marked the beginning of passionate social debates that still divide us. It changed ancient attitudes and boundary lines on matters both public and very private, from government to sex.

And now it has given us a president, Bill Clinton, who breathed that era's heady atmosphere, and inhaled deeply.

One sixties radical with second thoughts, Peter Collier, has written, "The stones we threw into the waters of our world in those days caused ripples that continue to lap on our shores today—for better and more often for worse."

It would be wrong to paint an entire generation—even those who nostalgically claim the sixties as their favorite decade—with a broad brush of the same color. Many survived and prevailed. As Marilyn Quayle remarked at the 1992 Republican National Convention in Houston, not all of her generation smoked dope, dropped out, and engaged in promiscuous sex. Not all bought into the feminist view that women are nothing without careers. "Women's lives are different from men's lives," she said. "We make different trade-offs. We make different sacrifices. And we get different rewards."

Mrs. Quayle said she thinks liberals are angry "because they believed the grandiose promises of the liberation movements. They're disappointed because most women do not wish to be liberated from their essential natures as women. Most of us love being mothers or wives, which gives our lives a richness that few men or women get from professional accomplishments alone. Nor has it made for a better society to liberate men from their obligations as husbands and fathers."

The culture of the sixties downplayed, ignored, or ridiculed such thinking, as today's culture does, but those who thought and think like Marilyn Quayle were able to survive and prevail in the sixties and no one can rob them of the fulfillment they have experienced.

Whatever their numbers, people who thought and lived as Mrs. Quayle has did not dominate the cultural debate or direction in the sixties. They are barely tolerated now by those who cannot come to grips with their own wrong choices and who treat the Marilyn Quayles of the world as a roadblock to the happiness that has eluded them, rather than as a directional signal to the road less traveled.

The intentions of sixties activists may have been good, their motives may have been noble, but history has shown that they made not just wrong personal decisions, but decisions that shook a nation to its foundation and created a fault line that has yet to be repaired.

No generation of Americans has ever made or heard more extravagant promises. Promises of revolution. Promises of utopia. Promises of ecstasy. Promises of justice. The agenda was nothing if not ambitious. The tragedy is that too many of these people have learned nothing from their broken promises. They continue to make new promises based on flawed assumptions, and they regularly break them. They are as unable to deliver on their promises today as they were when they were students.

To understand where the Baby Boomers want to take us, it is essential, as they once said, to understand where they are coming from. To understand why the promises they are making to us today won't work, it is crucial that we examine the promises they made before, which they broke.

The Promise of Liberation from the Traditional Family . . .

In the sixties, Betty Friedan, whose tome *The Feminine Mystique* was the guerrilla tract for large numbers of women, mocked the life of a mother and homemaker as consisting of "comfortable, empty, purposeless days." Such a life, chosen or not, wrote Friedan, doomed women to days of drudgery, making it impossible for them to "grow and realize one's full potential." Children and marriage were presented as the sworn enemy of self-fulfillment.

This was a generation that distrusted and was suspicious of its parents, and the feeling grew to be mutual. It is this generation, the one that didn't trust, and has not learned to trust, that now runs the country. As parental distrust and suspicion grew in the sixties, it was returned in even larger measure by those whose password phrase for entry into the counterculture was "Don't trust anyone over 30." Jim Morrison, lead singer for the Doors, always referred to his parents as "dead," though they were still alive.

The Promise of Unrestrained Expression . . .

"Little Richard's First Law of Youth Culture" set the agenda: Please kids by shocking their parents. Beyond popular culture, the artistic avant-garde threw off all convention in an effort to redefine art itself.

The Promise of Pharmaceutical Enlightenment . . .

Harvard's Dr. Timothy Leary, in *The Psychedelic Reader*, urged students to "tune in, turn on, drop out" as a surefire method of expanding their mental horizons. A quarter century of subsequent wholesale drug taking has dulled the senses and shortened the lives of millions of Americans.

The Promise of Sexual Freedom . . .

In 1966, Masters and Johnson shone the light of research into the dark corners of human sexuality. Everything was measured, categorized, and revealed. Most Americans were surprised to learn what went on in suburban bedrooms. The lesson drawn? "Do your own thing."

The Weathermen pursued their "Smash Monogamy" campaign. Committed couples were harangued until they admitted their "political errors" and split apart. The youth culture experimented with group sex and homosexuality out of a sense of political obligation.

The Promise of God's Death . . .

Activists, and even many theologians, sponsored an escape from traditional religion and morality in an attempt to create new values for a new generation. Abbie Hoffman commented, "God is dead and we did it for the kids."

The Promise to End Poverty . . .

In 1962, President John F. Kennedy delivered to Congress a message asking for the creation of a "public welfare program" designed to "attack dependency, juvenile delinquency, family breakdown, illegitimacy, ill health, and disability." In the Great Society that followed Kennedy's brief administration, the goals were expanded even further. Lyndon Johnson assured America, "The final conquest of poverty is within our grasp." This massive effort led one observer to comment, "God is dead, but fifty thousand social workers have risen to take His place."

The Promise of Preferential Treatment for the Young and the Strong . . .

The sixties generation's glorification of youth culture and belief that those under thirty possessed all the answers has led inevitably to the notion that older Americans and those who are infirm should "step aside." Medical professionals, as distinct from some very good and principled individual physicians, have become the new gods, ascribing to themselves the power to determine who should live and who should die. Even the unborn must live—and die—by their decisions.

The Promise of Progressive Education . . .

Students sought out—and found—courses without assignments, or lectures, or grades. Expressing their contempt for convention, they started the "Filthy Speech Movement," allowing wealthy, white kids the freedom to sound like teamsters and sailors.

Universities began to transform their most basic mission. Sociologist Robert Nisbet writes: "The ideologies which gained entry into the academy in the sixties claimed that the fundamental intellectual principles of Western culture were illegitimate and must be overthrown. With that destroyed, terms like truth, good, evil, and soul could be discarded."

The Promise That Bigger Government Will Do It All For You . . .

As the value of the individual declined, the power of government increased. Adopting a slogan much like McDonald's, government will now "do it all for you." Government is our keeper; we shall not want.

Government grows, yet problems do not shrink. Big Government has failed to solve the problems it has addressed because it cannot cure the causes of poverty, it can only address the symptoms, and it doesn't even do that well.

The attack on authority in the sixties was frontal and heavy. Jim Morrison spoke for many: "I have always been attracted to those ideas that were about revolt against authority . . . I am interested in anything about revolt, disorder, chaos—especially activity that seems to have no meaning. It seems to me to be the road to freedom."

The mottoes of the time, chanted with wild-eyed, unwashed intensity, tell the story: "If you see something slipping, push"; "Burn, baby, burn." Ancient concepts, known to Thomas Jefferson as "self-evident truths," including duty, personal honor and integrity, gentlemanly (or ladylike) conduct, loyalty, obligation, and the sacred were all disowned. The past was demolished, like a decaying, outdated building, to make way for a chrome-and-glass future. Paul Goodman, a leading theorist of the New Left, remarked, "For the first time the mention of country, community, place has lost its power to animate. Nobody but a scoundrel even tries it."

The sixties was judged, in its own time, by the height of

its aspirations. Today, it can be judged by the depth of its influence. When the evidence is weighed, the verdict is irrefutable: We have lived through the unfolding of its utter failure. Promises and illusions were shattered like glass. Americans are left to walk carefully among the jagged shards.

To fight poverty, the government has spent beyond the wildest dreams of Franklin D. Roosevelt. We've conducted a social experiment over three decades with $3.5 trillion in government funds, extracted from an overtaxed population. But it is never enough money. Poverty increases still because it is rooted not in the unconcern of a compassionate people, but in the remains of fragmented families. Welfare has proven a trap that eventually destroys the soul.

Feminist disdain for the family and the sexual revolution have given millions of women the "full potential" of abandonment and poverty and "liberated" countless children from the affection and care of their parents.

The results for adults have been deep sadness. Peter Collier recounts: "Two of my Movement comrades decided to get married. After a ceremony filled with gibberish about liberation and the Third World, there was a reception, featuring a large wedding cake frosted with the slogan, 'Smash Monogamy!' It occurred to me at the time that the newlyweds were like cannibals as they ate their cake, consuming their own future. Needless to say, their marriage didn't last long, leaving in its rubble a pair of pathetic children, whom I occasionally see walking around Berkeley looking like the survivors of an airplane disaster."

The results for children are more disturbing, because their suffering has been uninvited and undeserved. The Census Bureau estimates that only 39 percent of children born in 1988 will live with both parents until their eighteenth birthday. One study has concluded that ten years after their parents divorce, over 40 percent of children still have no set goals, possess only a limited education, and live with a sense of hopelessness. Psychologist Judith Wallerstein sums up, "Almost half of the chil-

dren enter adulthood as worried, underachieving, and sometimes angry young men and women."

The doctrine of the dispensable two-parent family—
enunciated in the sixties and still followed by too many
today—turned out to be a lie, and a particularly destructive
one. Those who embraced it have much to answer for. They
have sacrificed too many children on the altar of their ideology and self-interest.

"Enlightened" education has generally left students
entirely in the dark. Changes in higher education have left
many observers wondering, "What, precisely, is this higher
than?"

At Middlebury College in Vermont, you can take a class
called "Popular Culture, Eroticism, Aesthetics, Voyeurism,
and Misogyny in the Films of Brigitte Bardot." A class called
"Music Video 454," taught at California State University,
uses the *Rolling Stone Book of Rock Video* as its only textbook
and places students as extras in rock videos—for credit.

Is it any wonder that stories about the ignorance of college students have become clichéd? Recently, a Harvard
senior thanked his history professor for explaining World
War I, saying, "I never knew why people kept talking about a
second world war."

Professors who once were gateways to the learning of
previous times now have little left to teach. Their fields have
been impoverished by critical theories that reinterpret all
knowledge in terms of political and economic power and
exploitation. So they take up political causes as a profession,
using the classroom to organize for trendy goals. They
denounce injustice, but teach that objective rules of justice
are illusions.

J. Allen Smith, the father of many modern education
reforms, concluded in the end, "The trouble with us reformers is that we've made reform a crusade against all standards.
Well, we've smashed them all, and now neither we nor anybody else have anything left."

Artistic theories that hate beauty and order have undermined the meaning, value, and conscience of art. In popular culture, these theories have led to ever-stranger sins and more startling obscenities. Each year requires more baroque perversions to provoke a society's jaded capacity to feel outrage.

Frank Capra, director of some of the finest films ever made, walked away from the movie business at age sixty-four in the 1960s. He refused to adjust to the new order. In his 1971 autobiography, Capra wrote: "The winds of change blew through the dream factories. . . . The hedonists, the homosexuals, the hemophilic bleeding hearts, the God-haters, the quick-buck artists who substituted shock for talent, all cried, 'Shake 'em! Rattle 'em! God is dead. Long live Pleasure! Nudity? Yeah! Wife-swapping? Yeah! Liberate the world from prudery. Emancipate our films from morality!'"

In our "high" artistic culture, the transformation is equally stark. The National Endowment for the Arts, arbiter of the avant-garde, illustrates the change. In 1989, the NEA denied a modest request from the New York Academy of Art to provide young painters with skills in drawing the human figure. Susan Lubowsky, director of the NEA Visual Arts Program, explained, "Teaching students to draw the human figure is revisionist . . . and stifles creativity." The distinguished sculptor Frederick Hart, who created *Three Soldiers* at the Vietnam War Memorial, applied for a grant to do a series of sculptures. To his surprise, the Endowment turned him down. "The NEA told me I wasn't doing art," he said.

Yet in 1990, the NEA paid $70,000 to fund a show featuring Shawn Eichman's *Alchemy Cabinet*, which displayed a jar with the fetal remains from the "artist's" own abortion. Around the same time, it authorized $20,000 for a project in Lewiston, New York, whose goal was "to create large, sexually explicit props covered with a generous layer of requisitioned Bibles."

The escape from God and the triumph of secularism has

left many Americans with a feeling of isolation, confusion, and loneliness. They are disconnected from traditional sources of meaning, value, and love, like the family and the church. Sociologists call them "loose individuals"—free from traditional restraints, obsessed with self-fulfillment, but uncertain if anything makes much difference. They are sentenced, in the words of Malcolm Muggeridge, to "the dark little dungeon of the ego." Author George McDonald wrote, "The one principle of hell is, 'I am my own.'"

New York Times book critic Michiko Kakutani has written on the Boomers' preoccupation with the self: "What it does mean is that they're constantly assessing their happiness, monitoring their emotional damage.... And perhaps as a consequence they spend most of their time being miserable—lonely, isolated, and pretty much paralyzed when it comes to making decisions."

The ultimate result of all this is a genuine social crisis: a crisis of cultural authority. How can we make any moral judgments? "Who gives you the right to judge?" asks an angry reader of my columns. The question ought not be rhetorical. It demands an answer, but only those with a memory can give one that is satisfactory. How can we draw dividing lines between sane and insane, noble and base, beautiful and hideous, traitors and patriots? How can we know anything about living a good life? How can anyone cry for reform when "form" is without meaning?

Peter Collier and another former activist, David Horowitz, conclude: "In the inchoate attack against authority, we have weakened our culture's immune system, making it vulnerable to opportunistic diseases. The origins of metaphorical epidemics of crime and drugs could be traced to the sixties, as could literal ones such as AIDS."

The crisis has spread from the counterculture to the mainstream as a new generation takes positions of political and cultural leadership. The sixties saw no revolt of the oppressed, as some expected. It was a revolt of middle-class kids who got expensive educations. They chanted, "What Do We Want? Everything. When Do We Want It? Now!" But patience has given them advantages no sit-in could provide. They have gone on to become professors, pundits, politicians, even president. They seem intent on changing America into their image. They see themselves as the scouting party for a new world.

Where does this leave the rest of us? The promises of the sixties have been broken. They never could have been fulfilled, because they were based on wrong premises. Every victory claimed felt to most of us like defeat. But the children of the sixties often refuse to recognize that failure. Perhaps that is why *Rolling Stone* magazine found in a massive survey of the "Baby Boomers" that this pampered generation has more of its members on the psychiatrist's couch than any other in history.

The flower children cling to their promises as a shield against the facts, pushing their own agenda to its (and our) limits. In desperation, every extreme they perpetrate looks to them like one last chance to reverse the verdict of history. So government still grows, though the benefits are slim for such a massive investment. The family is attacked as a form of slavery, while children find broken lives in broken homes. Grade schoolers are taught to be sex experts, as though that will save them from the consequences of permissiveness. New ways are discovered to shock the bourgeoisie, who are increasingly immune to shock.

When on a university campus someone raises the lonely voice of opposition, he is often simply gagged. Conservative speakers are shouted down—in the increasingly rare instances where they are invited to speak. Compassion and tolerance turn quickly into hatred and intolerance. "Speech codes" declare certain politically incorrect ideas off-limits for discussion. Roger Kimball, editor of the *New Criterion*, argues, "At a time when student populations at many colleges and universities are becoming increasingly conservative, it is nothing less than an effort by left-leaning faculties and administrations to impose the politics and mind-set of the sixties by fiat."

The revolution of the sixties—once intended as a crisis for others—has found a crisis of its own. If a cultural crimes trial were to be convened, like the war crimes trials of the past, the testimony of victims would be damning. An abandoned child. An overdosed teenager. A trapped welfare mother. An ignorant student. A young woman with venereal disease, or worse. Each could ask, in a pained voice, "Where was my liberation? When do we arrive at the Age of Aquarius where harmony and understanding, sympathy and trust abound?"

At this moment of reckoning, America has elected its first president who was shaped and motivated by the sixties. He embodies that decade, with all its attractiveness and blindness. When he moved into the White House, he brought with him all the hope and baggage of an era.

What would a composite sketch of a sixties president look like? He would have been drafted to fight in Vietnam, but still managed to avoid service.

He would have helped organize demonstrations in a foreign country against U.S. involvement in that war.

He would have visited the Oslo Peace Institute to talk with conscientious objectors.

He would have experimented with drugs and later dismissed his lawbreaking as unimportant. He would say on MTV, when asked whether he would inhale if he had it to do over again: "Sure, if I could. I tried before."

He would be the Texas coordinator for George McGovern's presidential bid.

He would marry a radical activist who helped edit the *Yale Review of Law and Social Action*, which would run cartoons of decapitated and dismembered pigs, representing the police, paired with the caption, "Seize the day."

He would show contempt for family commitments through his admitted and unrepentant infidelity.

He would sponsor, as governor, a tax-funded summer

school for high school seniors that would experiment with a radical curriculum. It would require the study of an essay that describes Jesus' teachings as "inescapably hierarchical" and his death on the cross as "necrophilic and sadomasochistic." It would include a lesson on animal rights that compares chicken harvesting to the Holocaust. It would include a lecture from the attorney for "Jane Roe" in *Roe* v. *Wade*.

Bob Dylan sang, at the height of the sixties, "Something is happening here, but you don't know what it is. Do you, Mister Jones?" Bill Clinton knew precisely what was happening. He placed himself in the thick of it. He believed in it, was part of it, accepted and articulated its promises.

Jerry Rubin, in his book *Do It!*, predicted a "Youth International Revolution" staged by "tribes of longhairs, armed women, workers, peasants, and students." The White House was slated to "become one big commune." The Pentagon "will be replaced with an LSD experimental farm."

The Clinton White House is not the kind of commune Rubin imagined. But the promises and priorities of the sixties were unmistakably present during the president's first months in office.

There is more here than Jefferson Airplane at the Democratic convention and Peter, Paul, and Mary at the Inaugural Gala. "Don't stop thinking about tomorrow" means you never have to think about the present, the only moment in history in which we are sure of living and the only moment in time when we can have an impact on our world.

We have seen, so far from the Clinton administration, a concrete, broad agenda, informed by the radicalism of the past. Billions of dollars in proposed new social spending (much of it taken from the military, which the sixties generation loathed). Homosexuals in the military (pushed mostly by those in leadership with no military experience). Massive defense cuts. Paying for abortion counseling with government funds. Promoting fetal tissue research and the abortion pill RU-486. Appointing an openly lesbian activist for homosexual adoption to a high position at the Department of Housing and Urban Development, and aggressively hiring homosexuals and celebrating "gay pride" events throughout government.

In one way, this is disturbing, or ought to be. We seem condemned to repeat all the failures of a destructive generation. But the Clinton presidency also serves an important purpose: It requires our nation to make a choice.

We cannot believe ourselves to be the virtuous, religious republic of our history yet act according to the secular, libertine vision of the sixties. The tension is too great. One image of ourselves as a nation must fade.

F. Scott Fitzgerald wrote, "France was a land, England a people, but America, having about it still that quality of idea, was harder to utter." The content of that idea, since the sixties, has become uncertain. In this decade, we will see a fundamental choice on who speaks the language of American ideals. The choice we make will shape us far into the twenty-first century.

PART ONE

"I'M GOING HOME"

Ten Years After, Woodstock

CHAPTER 1

The Promise of Liberation from the Traditional Family

"Married: Tom Hayden, 53, former radical student leader, ex-husband of Jane Fonda and current California state senator, and Barbara Williams, 40, actress; in Tofino, British Columbia. The couple were married by a Buddhist priest. Wedding vows included a passage in which the pair committed themselves to the preservation of old-growth forests."

TIME MAGAZINE
AUGUST 23, 1993

Marriage has taken a beating in the last thirty years. Even *Woman's Day*, once considered a magazine for "homemakers," has published a "marriage contract" that couples can sign before the wedding. It's the type of do-it-yourself prenuptial agreement that offers couples the opportunity to jettison one another if things "don't work out."

"No-fault" divorces, lesbian and gay "marriages," adoption of children by homosexual couples—along with the daily pressures on married life brought on by double-wage earning and decline in cultural support for matrimony—has brought marriages once thought to be made in heaven to the edge of hell, where they are easily torn apart.

For three thousand years, marriage was considered one of humanity's most civilized rituals and institutions. In *The Odyssey*, Homer articulated a belief about marriage that was widely shared, if not always practiced, by most civilized human beings: "There is nothing nobler or more admirable than when two people who see eye-to-eye keep house as man and wife, confounding their enemies and delighting their friends."

Until recently, marriage was largely thought of as a noble relationship, not an "institution"—the word used with such glee by comedians. Lately, though, the general cynicism that dilutes and corrupts nearly everything it touches has spoiled even the idea of marriage for many.

Writing in the September 20, 1993, issue of *Time* magazine, essayist Barbara Ehrenreich uses the breakup of the supposedly "picture-perfect" marriage of actors Burt Reynolds and Loni Anderson to say that we expect too much from marriage and ought to revise the system and our expectations of it.

"To put the whole thing in an anthropological perspective," she writes, "what we lack is not 'values' but old-fashioned neighborhood or community. Once people found companionship among their old high school buddies and got help with child raising from granddads and aunts. Marriages lasted because less was expected of them. If you wanted a bridge partner or plumber or confidant, you had a whole village to choose from. Today we don't marry a person—i.e., a flawed and limited human being—we attempt to marry a village. . . ."

So far, a pretty fair analysis of how marriage has evolved. But Ehrenreich goes on to offer a perplexing remedy: ". . . The solution is to have separate 'marriages' for separate types of marital functions. For example, a gay man of my acquaintance has entered into a co-parenting arrangement with two lesbian women. He will be a father to their collective child without any expectations that he will be a lover to the child's mothers or, for that matter, a jogging companion or co-mortgage holder. Child raising, in other words, has cleanly been separated from the turbulent realm of sex, which can only be good for the child. Or consider my relationship with the plumber. He dashes over loyally whenever a pipe bursts, but there is no expectation of sex or profound emotional sharing. Consequently, ours is a 'marriage' that works."

Contrary to Barbara Ehrenreich's view, for many there remains something purposeful and energizing about marriage. Writing in the May 15, 1993, issue of the British magazine *The Spectator*, Paul Johnson sees the first light of a new dawn in which marriage may again be affirmed and widely practiced and preserved. Part of that reason, he notes, is the "hard knocks" marriage has recently sustained.

"First," says Johnson, "there has been that grotesque and hostile parody of marriage which has been enacted in a Manhattan courtroom, as Mia Farrow and Woody Allen, each flanked by platoons of lawyers, shrinks, and counselors, and watched by strings of wide-eyed, silent, reproachful children, both adopted and (as they say) biological, have hurled accusations of cruelty, incest, betrayal, and madness at each other. The case has attracted huge interest even over here: Men and women I know have taken sides, often quite violently. In a way, all the modern age and its secularist, faithless, psychiatrist's values have been on trial in the courtroom, and a disgusted world has pronounced a unanimous verdict: Guilty!"

Sadly, there are few high-profile happy, healthy marriages that can be held up to convince others that this is a lifestyle worth entering into and valuable enough to preserve.

Still, what else is there? Despite its sometime problems, most people would prefer the depth of a marital relationship to the comparative superficiality of living together, living alone, or trying to relate to a pet.

Paul Johnson writes that the "extraordinary thing about this revival of marriage is that it runs directly counter to the whole spirit of the age. All the resources and provisions of the welfare state, the injunctions of political correctness, the weight of academic opinion, the advice of tax accountants, the verdicts of the courts, and the direction of new legislation . . . combine to suggest that marriage today is not merely unnecessary, expensive, evidence of heterosexual triumphalism and homophobia, old-fashioned, reactionary, Thatcherite, and suburban, but legally perilous too."

That marriage may be making a comeback in spite of all these obstacles may be due to the growing realization that while a good marriage cannot *guarantee* happy, socially well-adjusted children, it does increase the odds.

DAN QUAYLE REVISITED

Famous family values advocate Vice President Dan Quayle took a lot of flak for linking successful marriages with successful child rearing in what has become known as the "Murphy Brown Speech." Time has since vindicated him. In an April 1993 *Atlantic* cover story, "Dan Quayle Was Right," writer Barbara Dafoe Whitehead states: "According to a growing body of social-scientific evidence, children in families disrupted by divorce and out-of-wedlock birth do worse than children in intact families on several measures of well-being."

And how does Whitehead define "worse"? Worse in terms of family income. Worse in terms of teenage pregnancies and dropping out of school, drug abuse, and crime. Among Whitehead's findings:

• Children in single-parent families are six times as likely to be poor.

• Children in single-parent families are two to three times as likely as children in two-parent families to have emotional and behavioral problems. They are also more likely to drop out of high school, to get pregnant as teenagers, to abuse drugs, and to be in trouble with the law.

• The out-of-wedlock birthrate in 1990 was 27 percent—a huge jump from the five percent rate in 1960. Altogether, more than one out of every four women who had a child in 1990 was not married.

As the body of evidence grows that the sixties flower children have sown the seeds that produced a breakdown of the family, we hear only a grudging admission, not the apology that is due the country—and certainly not any suggestion that we should turn back on this road that has led to cultural destruction and take another one leading to healing and restoration.

"Coping" remains the key word. Supermarket checkout magazines continue their fiction of the liberated divorced woman with children. Trouble is, most of these "liberated" women (like ABC's Joan Lunden, who has appeared on several magazine covers in articles about her divorce from her producer-husband) are financially well-off. They do not represent most American women, for whom a drastically reduced income and lifestyle, and often poverty, result from the breakup of their marriages.

Increasingly the tactic of apologists from the sixties generation's "if it feels good, do it" approach is to ask, "What are 'family values'?" and "What is a 'family'?"

The debate over families and family values generally finds advocates in two camps. One camp says that a family begins when a man and a woman legally marry. (Families also would include widowed or divorced people and extended families that might be made up of grandparents or guardians. But the beginning of the family could be traced back to the marriage of a man and a woman.)

The other camp says that no one should try to define the family because people disagree on a definition and some might be unfairly excluded.

This latter position is just one example of the virus that has caused America's sickness. We have abandoned a standard for objective truth and the process by which it might be discovered.

The idea that a fixed standard cannot be established because some people might disagree does not apply to weights and measures. Imagine the chaos if every supermarket decided for itself what was a pound, a quart, or a liter, and each one came up with different standards according to its own methods of measuring.

The argument that there should be no fixed standards in the family and moral arenas is unevenly applied by those who make it. Logic tells us that if there is no objective standard for one agenda, there can be none for any other. In fact, the

Left has universal standards based on "truths" it considers politically correct: from welfare, to universal health care, to high taxes for "the rich"; from civil rights for all—including homosexuals, whom they consider a bona fide minority—to no censorship for pornography, but censorship for religion.

But the possibility of "standards" or "truths" is conveniently forgotten when the situation warrants.

As the late philosopher Francis Schaeffer wrote in his book *How Should We Then Live?*, "Pragmatism, doing what seems to work without regard to fixed principles of right or wrong, is largely in control. In both international and home affairs, expediency—at any price to maintain personal peace and affluence at the moment—is the accepted procedure. Absolute principles have little or no meaning in the place to which the decline of Western thought has come."

If divorce or abortion or any other behavior can be indulged in without people being held accountable to a standard that society deems in the best interests of everyone, why should anyone be concerned about the rights of others, or justice, or equality? If we are all on a grand evolutionary course (as Darwinists assert), then survival of the fittest becomes our creed, not appeals to things "noble," whatever that may mean.

Following this line of wrongheaded thinking, I can go ahead and abort my child or divorce my wife as long as it makes me "happy," even in the short term (no matter how miserable I or others may be in the long term). That is all that should matter.

The debate in our culture in the nineties is whose values, whose philosophy, whose moral vision for America, and whose idea of "family" will prevail. That is what underlies the talk about "family values." The resolution of that debate will determine whether we will have to apologize to our grandparents for our poor stewardship of the nation we must deliver to our grandchildren.

ANOTHER DAN,
BUT THE SAME CONCLUSION

Another Dan, Senator Daniel Patrick Moynihan, New York Democrat, said nearly thirty years ago some of the same things that Dan Quayle said in 1992. He, too, challenged a domestic social order that had turned the wreckage of family breakups into a major industry. He, too, argued the crucial importance of stable marriages, especially among the poor.

Senator Moynihan said in the sixties, when he was a young assistant in the Lyndon Johnson administration, "From the wild Irish slums of the nineteenth-century Eastern seaboard to the riot-torn suburbs of Los Angeles, there is one unmistakable lesson in American history: A community that allows a large number of young men to grow up in broken families, dominated by women, never acquiring any set of rational expectations about the future—that community asks for and gets chaos."

Moynihan suffered the most extreme form of criticism. He was called a racist by those who used the word to avoid debate on the substance of his remarks. Moynihan challenged the prevailing view among intellectual and social elites that "Negroes" (as blacks, or African-Americans, were then called) had been so affected by the slavery of their ancestors that they bore a type of mark of Cain which would remain with them forever and that it was incumbent upon white America to pay reparations in the form of government checks to all blacks who are poor—thus ensuring they remain so.

Moynihan was right then and so was Dan Quayle in 1992.

In the aforementioned "Murphy Brown Speech," Dan Quayle hit a raw nerve when he said, "I believe the lawless social anarchy which we saw [in the Los Angeles riots following the state trial of the police officers involved in beating Rodney King] is directly related to the breakdown of family structure, personal responsibility, and social order in too many areas of our society."

How could anyone argue with this? But many do, because to acknowledge the legitimacy of such a diagnosis would require those who unleashed this plague on the country to take responsibility for it. And if the sixties taught these people anything, it was to avoid responsibility and accountability at all costs. For them, as Rush Limbaugh has commented about President Clinton, the buck doesn't stop here; the buck never gets here at all.

In order to avoid discussing Quayle's conclusions (and those of Daniel Patrick Moynihan, for that matter), many liberals misrepresented his comments. They tried to convince the public that Quayle believed a situation comedy, "Murphy Brown," which seemed to advocate single parenthood, had caused the social fabric to unravel.

Yet Quayle's figures, which were ignored in the reporting and editorializing on his speech, were exactly on target. Since 1965, the fastest-growing segment of the poor has been single mothers and their children under age eighteen. Illegitimacy rates in some poverty areas surpass 80 percent. And with so many single mothers having to "cope" by themselves, children are getting far less supervision—a situation that has had tragic consequences.

The irony is that most Americans remain philosophically in accord with the former vice president's assessment of the problem. Trouble is, they do not set the "American Agenda." The elite does.

NO LONGER HOME ALONE

Though they are frequently powerless to influence the larger course of events, people can and do tailor their individual actions according to an instinctive belief about what is happening. A growing number of professional women, for example (according to a recent Labor Department report), are quitting paid work and choosing to live at home with their young children. While some can no longer take the pressures of managing both a career and motherhood, many simply find greater fulfillment in helping to rear a child who will be successful in life than in the dubious and short-term rewards that come from succeeding at a job.

Not only are many women finding it not worth it, so are young children. Psychologist Brenda Hunter, who holds a doctorate from Georgetown University, believes that America's children feel adrift and homeless. Hunter is especially concerned about children who are put in day-care centers while they are still infants. "Those who—the research shows—feel rejected by their mothers and sometimes by their fathers" are increasing, she says.

In her book, *Home by Choice: Facing the Effects of Mother's Absence*, Hunter writes of her concern "about a culture that is at war against mother love. For more than two decades we have made it costly for women to elect to stay at home to nurture their children, and those who have chosen home have paid dearly both economically and in terms of self-esteem."

Hunter indicts feminist leaders like Gloria Steinem, Germaine Greer, and Betty Friedan, who, she says, are products of dysfunctional families and who are rebelling against the poor nurturing she says they experienced as children. Because of their own inadequate childhood experiences, says Hunter, they have led women to make wrong choices that have adversely affected their lives as well as the lives of their children.

Betty Friedan, writes Hunter, "grew up in a household short on mother love. According to Betty's sister, Amy, their mother, Marian, had a 'complete inability to nurture. . . . We really absolutely did not have a mother loving us.'" Similar stories are recounted of the upbringing of Steinem and Greer.

Hunter says that a child internalizes a sense of "home" or an abiding sense of "homelessness" based on those earliest parental attachments, and that the mother is central in this process. If a mother is often absent or emotionally inaccessible, a child may suffer profound consequences.

Reading Hunter—indeed, just observing popular culture—reveals the lies that women have been told, about themselves, about relationships, about sex, about, as Marilyn Quayle said at the Republican National Convention in Houston in 1992, "our essential nature as women." By skillful manipulation, a generation of women (and men, too) has been led to believe that ultimate fulfillment is to be found in the workplace and not in cooperation with men, successfully rearing the next generation.

"Children are the anchors that hold a mother to life," wrote Sophocles. Nothing has substantially changed since he penned those words, except that many women have raised their anchors and set out for other ports. The shipwrecks that litter the landscape are testimony to how far off course many have gone.

ANOTHER ONE BITES THE DUST:
FILM AT 11

The lesson that chaos will result if parents are not around to give direction to their children's lives is one that is reinforced each night on the local news.

In Washington, D.C., where I live, the 11 P.M. news is a never-ending docudrama of killings and mayhem in which tales of woe—many of them perpetrated by teenage hoodlums—dominate.

A local radio reporter, J. J. Green, recently interviewed several convicted murderers to see if he could learn what motivates them to kill.

One of those interviewed was seventeen-year-old Eudon Bernard, who was only fifteen when he shot and killed a man. The written transcript of Green's interview cannot fully convey the cold, matter-of-fact detachment of Bernard's voice.

"There was nothing going through my mind while I was pumping," explained Bernard, who says he shot his victim six times with a .357 Magnum. Bernard said he had heard his target was trying to get him so he decided, in a perversion of the Golden Rule, to get him first.

"I walked up to him and stuck the gun in him and shot him," said Bernard with no remorse. "He tried to move out of the way of the bullets, but I got him before he could. Then I ran back to the car and pulled off."

Then–police chief Isaac Fulwood told Green that more than drug abuse is responsible for the violence in America's cities. "You can watch police shows or any other kind of show on television," said Fulwood. "There's a mindless thing about it. Parents don't watch their kids and screen what they see."

Isaac Fulwood is also concerned about the lack of contrition in a growing number of criminals: "In my personal conversations with young people who have been involved with violence, there is no remorse. There's not the first tear. There's no sense that shooting another human being is wrong. Any police officer will tell you that when they go to the suspect's house to make an arrest, they're often in bed sleeping just like it was any other day. We have police officers who retire when they shoot people; the stress gets to them. How come these people feel nothing?"

They feel nothing largely because they have nothing to feel. Almost without exception, these young criminals come from homes without love, without nurturance, without role models, and without hope.

Cynthia Harris, whose son was murdered in 1988 in Washington, told Green, "We erred when we began to look at law enforcement as the only means to solve the problem [of violence] and to look at the drug crisis as our only problem."

She's right. The jails and prisons are full, and the rehabilitation programs don't rehabilitate. The recidivism rate remains around 70 percent. And the problem grows worse, because too many people continue to pretend that the old "solutions" (which only solved problems in the minds of those who came up with them) can be made to work given more time, more studies, and, of course, more tax money.

No politician, no spending program, is going to be able to stop any of this. Only a decision by millions of parents to reverse course and put their families first will do it. An intact family is the greatest anticrime weapon available. We have enough history now to prove that nothing else works.

"LITTLE BIG PEOPLE"

On October 10, 1993, the *New York Times Magazine* ran a cover story entitled: "Little Big People." The tag line read: "They're precocious, even out of control, and their affluent parents have only themselves to blame."

The story, by Pulitzer Prize–winning journalist Lucinda Franks, is a devastating commentary on the anti-values generation that has produced, in Frank's words, ". . . a crop of under-12's, particularly in middle- and upper-middle-income families and particularly in urban America, (that) seems to have reinvented—or even bypassed—childhood as we knew it."

Franks points out that her generation's idea of childhood "was like everything else: radically different from our parents', who thought a child was just a child, even when the child got old enough to march against wars and otherwise protest the way the elder generation ran the world. Those of us who were veterans of the sixties and seventies swore that we would treat our children with respect. We vowed that we would fold our own offspring into our daily lives, treating them like 'little people,' empowering them with the rights, the importance, and the truth-telling we had been denied. We wanted to create the children we always yearned to be.

"And now, many years later, we are confronted with the results. Did it turn out the way we meant it to? Will our independent children thank us for making them the center of the universe, or have we robbed them of a childhood they can never regain?"

The evidence clearly indicates we may have done just that.

In Montgomery County, Maryland, in the wealthy Washington, D.C., suburbs, several parents rented a bus so that their young teenage children could go to underage drinking parties. This was supposed to protect them (and us) from their driving drunk. One of the mothers was quoted in press reports as saying that parents must allow their children to attend these parties, some of which are raided by the police, because they want to, and that if they are refused permission "they might leave home."

I say, let them go and tell them to write when they find food! These parents should listen to Lucinda Franks, who wrote, "We have abrogated the moral authority our parents wore as easily as gloves." Franks writes of some Westchester County, New York, parents who are much like those in Maryland. She says they are afraid to tell their children not to go into New York City to drinking parties or to abide by curfews because they might leave home and live with a friend.

As teenagers, many of the Boomers rebelled against authority. Now their children are rebelling against the *lack* of authority, and the absence of boundaries inside which they may safely live and play. They are rebelling because of the absence of *parents*, whose careers and causes have become their real children.

Kids don't really want to live this way. One third-grader quoted in the Franks article was asked to list questions he had during a sex education course. One of them was, "Why do we have to know about stuff like this?" Good question. What he is really asking is, Why don't you let us alone and allow us to be children?

THE GAY NINETIES

The gay rights movement exploded in the eighties and early nineties to present perhaps the strongest challenge to the traditional male-female family structure in history.

Homosexuals dominate the broadcast and print media. Their worldview, that they are as normal as heterosexuals, that God made them the way they are and that they cannot change, is the starting point for all debates on the subject. It is rare, however, that there is a debate. Most of the television networks offer one-sided presentations that more closely resemble propaganda than journalism.

Homosexuals are now desperately searching for a silver bullet. They think they'll find it in their genes. That most of the "research" in this field is conducted either by homosexuals or by those who begin with an objective and an agenda and try to skewer science to achieve them (a distinctly unscientific method) is completely lost on media interrogators, who treat this "research" as legitimate and acceptable.

One of the major scientific gurus in this battle to win acceptance for the gay lifestyle is Dr. Simon LeVay, a neurologist at the Salk Institute in La Jolla, California.

LeVay says he is a homosexual. On any other issue this would be seen as a liability. When Dr. Bernard Nathanson did abortions at the nation's largest abortion clinic in New York, he was sought after as an expert. When he converted to the pro-life side, he was ignored and his positions were ridiculed by those who had once regarded him as knowledgeable. With homosexuality, as with abortion, politics leads the way for science.

LeVay examined the brains of homosexual men, all of whom had died of AIDS, and the brains of men presumed to have been heterosexual, some of whom died of AIDS through intravenous drug use and some of whom died from other causes. He reported in *Science* magazine that the hypothalamus portion of the brain in the homosexual men was only a quarter of the size of the same region in the heterosexual men.

LeVay cautioned against reaching firm conclusions about these differences until further studies are done, but that didn't stop some in the gay rights community and the press. It was front-page news in many newspapers, and the television networks covered it as if it were a definitive discovery.

Nowhere was it reported that LeVay's theory is an old one, which had been rejected by scientists in the past.

In his book *Reparative Theory of Male Homosexuality: A New Clinical Approach*, Joseph Nicolosi, Ph.D., founder and clinical director of the Thomas Aquinas Psychological Clinic in Encino, California, examines some of these studies.

Nicolosi says he "treats homosexual men who are trying to change." And he makes a crucial and interesting distinction between homosexuals, "a name that is an undeniable part of their psychology," and gay, "which describes a lifestyle and values [homosexuals] do not claim."

Nicolosi cites substantial scientific evidence confirming that hormonal and genetic factors "do not seem to play a determining role in homosexuality." Despite this evidence, he says, there continue to be attempts to prove that genetics rather than family factors determines sexual direction. "Those continuing efforts reflect the persistence of gay advocates to formulate a means by which homosexual behavior may be viewed as normal."

LeVay's references to animal research, in which it was learned that injury to the hypothalamus in the brains of rats and monkeys causes males to lose interest in females while continuing to express sexual vigor in other ways, was also dismissed by Nicolosi.

"Physiogenetic research," he writes, "can be divided into two categories—human studies and animal studies. A few of the human studies have reported hormonal differences between homosexual and heterosexual men, but little convincing evidence has been found. In addition, these studies are extremely lacking in consistency and replication of findings."

In fact, according to W. Gadpaille, writing in the *Archives of General Psychiatry* in 1980, "Preferential homosexuality is not found naturally in any infrahuman mammalian species. Masculine/feminine differences and heterosexual preferences are quite consistent up through the phylogenetic (development) stage."

Those who hold the view that the way a child is nurtured plays more of a role than biology in that child's choosing a gay lifestyle are in line with the conclusions of R. Gundlach, who wrote in the *Journal of Consulting and Clinical Psychology* in 1969, "In the light of evidence of cultural determination of gender role and sexual practices, the possibility of an innate physical/sexual characteristic determining homosexuality seems quite remote."

Nicolosi gets to the heart of the debate over gay rights when he writes, "The question of a biological basis for homosexuality has been reopened due to pressure for minority-rights status for homosexuals. Justification for this special civil rights status would be supported if scientific evidence could be found that homosexuality is inborn. . . . The more deeply identified a person is with his sexual orientation, the more he prefers to believe it was prenatally determined."

The reason so many are confused as to what they should believe about homosexuality is because the country has lost its moral compass. Those who oppose the gay rights agenda are labeled "homophobic," but gays are "moralphobic," because they fear and reject an objective moral code.

The question about choice and homosexuality is often asked the wrong way. It is not so much that one chooses to engage in homosexual acts as it is that one can choose not to. We are all predisposed to some things, and frequently tempted. But we make choices every day not to engage in certain activities, for any number of reasons. The power not to make certain choices is available to one who is tempted to engage in homosexual acts (or heterosexual acts outside of marriage).

As for the argument often heard from the gay community about twins and the significant percentage of twins who are homosexual, most studies I've read supporting the biological view do not consider factors other than genetics. Influences such as interest in art, music, or dance (which can lead to ridicule in school from the more macho athletic types), the absence (physical and/or emotional) of a father or father figure, and sexual molestation can contribute to a person's desire (or the desire by twins) to seek the sexual companionship of a person of the same gender.

Logically, if genetics alone determined homosexual behavior, all homosexuals who have twin brothers or sisters would find them also to be homosexual. But they are not, so it is difficult to believe that genetics alone can be the "cause" of homosexuality among some twins.

Some contend that homosexual acts must be normal because no one would "choose" a lifestyle that brings such alienation. The answer to that is that the drive to engage in homosexual acts and the short-term fulfillment many feel outweighs for them the social ostracism they may experience. Is this not human nature? How many in prison seriously weighed the consequences of the possible penalties of their decisions before engaging in criminal behavior? How many who take up smoking are dissuaded by reading the warning label on the cigarette package or considering scientific studies that indicate they might contract lung cancer or heart disease?

The good news for homosexuals, even gays, who want to change is that they can. But one must first have the desire. The road to true gay liberation is not through the hypothalamus, but in changed ways of thinking and behaving. I have a number of friends who were once part of the gay lifestyle.

Many are now married to people of the opposite gender and enjoying a new life. They are the best "scientific" evidence that people who can change are not deserving of special "civil rights" consideration and shouldn't be recognized as part of a wider and redefined family.

THE WORLD TRADE CENTER BOMBING AND THE MEANING OF LIFE

When New York's World Trade Center was bombed by a group of radical Moslems in the winter of 1993, it served as a symbol for the jarring of more critical foundations not far away in the city's Municipal Building. One hundred and nine couples showed up to register as "domestic partners" under a new city law that grants rights previously reserved for heterosexual couples who legally marry. Now, a special status is available to heterosexual or homosexual "partners" who wish to live together without, as we once quaintly put it, benefit of clergy, though these days you could find "clergy" who would "marry" a human to his dog.

For $20, the domestic partners receive their long-sought societal approval. What was once considered a "sin" is now deemed acceptable behavior.

Domestic partners employed by the city of New York are now eligible for the same health and sick-leave benefits as married couples, thus forcing those who deem such arrangements immoral to subsidize behavior they find abhorrent.

We can't say we weren't warned this was coming. As long ago as 1970, at a homosexual convention in Philadelphia, delegates called for "the abolition of the nuclear family because it perpetuates the false categories of homosexuality and heterosexuality." A lesbian workshop demanded the "destruction of the nuclear family," which a statement called "a microcosm of the fascist state."

More than a century ago, the Supreme Court defined a family as beginning when a man and woman legally marry. But given the evolutionary principle now at work in the law, it is possible we shall live to see this definition redefined.

Since the last century, the Supreme Court has consistently refused to sanction polygamy, bigamy, or any other relationship that would define a family as beginning outside of male-female marriage. It has called the marital bond between husband and wife "the true basis of human progress."

In *Griswold* v. *Connecticut* (1965), the court said, "Marriage is a coming together for better or for worse, hopefully enduring, and intimate to the degree of being sacred. It is an association that promotes a way of life."

The "domestic partner" arrangement also promotes a way of life—a way of life that is an assault on the most important building block of any society: the traditional concept of family.

In his once widely read *Commentaries on the Laws of England* (originally published in 1765), legal scholar William Blackstone saw law as coming from a Creator who not only endowed humans with certain rights, but also established rules for a social order that, if followed, would profit individuals and society.

"Man, considered as a creature," wrote Blackstone, "must necessarily be subject to the laws of his Creator, for he is an entirely dependent being." Blackstone said the will of man's Maker is "the law of nature" and "this law of nature, being co-equal with mankind and dictated by God himself, is of course superior in obligation to any other . . . no human laws are of any validity, if contrary to this."

In New York City and in other cities and states, and even at the federal level, many lawmakers in effect have declared themselves to be God and are busy assisting in the destruction of the one foundation of law and nature that has held us up for more than two centuries. The destruction of *this* foundation will cause more damage than a single bombing at the World Trade Center.

PART TWO

"SEA OF MADNESS"

Crosby, Stills, Nash & Young, Woodstock

CHAPTER 2

The Promise of Unrestrained Expression

Some historical revisionists, children of the sixties, are busy putting a new spin on their generation.

E. J. Dionne, Jr., of the *Washington Post*, wrote in the April 13, 1993, issue of that newspaper, "Liberals need to realize that sixties nostalgia only feeds conservative reaction against the real achievements of the era. Conservatives pick up on the silliest things that were said or thought back then—about the family, about violence, about the work ethic, about personal responsibility—and then pray that liberals will make themselves look dumb by leaping to the defense."

Contrary to the assertions of Mr. Dionne, it is not just what was *said* in the sixties about the family, about violence, about the work ethic, about personal responsibility; it is what was *done*. That's the thing about "expression." It doesn't exist in a vacuum. The thoughts and words are father to the deeds. And deeds, as we all know, sometimes have very serious consequences.

THE SCHOTT HEARD 'ROUND THE WORLD

When a Florida jury decided that the rap group 2 Live Crew did not violate local obscenity laws with its *As Nasty as They Wanna Be* recording, the very idea of obscenity as a concept that can be objectively defined evaporated. If *As Nasty ...*, with its grotesque sexual and violent content, isn't obscene, then nothing is.

How obscene was it? One reviewer catalogued the variety of sexually explicit language, which included the following:

- 226 uses of the "F" word
- 117 explicit terms for male and female genitalia
- 87 descriptions of oral sex
- 163 uses of "bitch"
- 15 uses of "ho" (slang for whore) when referring to women
- 81 uses of "shit"
- 42 uses of "ass"
- 9 descriptions of male ejaculation
- 4 descriptions of group sex
- more than a dozen references to violent sex

Anyone who seriously believes that people can regularly listen to swill like this and not be affected by it—indeed, that a few already warped minds would not be prompted to act out the suggestions contained in it—must be deluded. The increases in violent sexual assault and sexual harassment against women must come from somewhere. One doesn't need to be a sociologist to see the connection between "music" like this and the permission it gives some people who are predisposed to such behavior to try it out on a woman they know (or on one they don't know).

Though the Florida court refused to declare the words obscene, there is some language that is considered politically obscene, depending on who says it and to whom it is said. Black rap groups can say whatever they wish, even employing the racially pejorative word "nigger," and suffer no consequences. They can call women "bitches" and suggest that they be cut with knives in their private parts, and this is supposed to be the price we pay for a "healthy" First Amendment.

But such freedom is denied to others, as campus speech codes have demonstrated (thankfully ruled unconstitutional by the Supreme Court, although other forms of "political correctness" remain in force), and as the owner of the Cincinnati Reds baseball team learned the hard way.

Marge Schott was not accused of making public remarks that were offensive to most people. She was overheard in a private telephone conversation in which it was alleged she demeaned blacks, Jews, and people of Japanese ancestry. The person overhearing her made sure the press found out about it and Schott was officially disciplined, though not severely, by baseball management.

In 1987, Al Campanis, then of the Los Angeles Dodgers, committed political hari-kari when he said on ABC's "Nightline" that the reason there were not more black managers in baseball was because there was something inherent in their race that kept them from becoming management material.

That Campanis was wrong is not the issue in the free-speech debate. Did he have a right to his opinion, as wrong-headed as it is? Not in the nineties, he doesn't. And neither does Marge Schott, even in a private conversation. Yet, Rev. Jesse Jackson can call Jews "Hymies" and New York City "Hymietown" and he loses neither an income-producing job nor his stature in the political and media communities (though some editorial writers criticized Jackson for his remarks and Jackson was forced to issue one of those "If I've offended anyone . . ." apologies).

With respect to free expression, it seems that we live in the Age of the Double Standard. While people of religious faith, for example, are frequently slandered and stereotyped, members of politically correct groups are given carte blanche to voice their opinions. Witness talk show host Arsenio Hall's response during the 1992 campaign when then–White House Press Secretary Marlin Fitzwater said President Bush would probably not appear on Hall's show: "Excuse me, George Herbert, irregular-heart-beating, read-my-lying-lipping, slip-ping-in-the-polls, do-nothing, deficit-raising, make-less-money-than-Millie-the-White-House-dog-did-last-year, Quayle-loving, sushi-puking Bush. I don't remember inviting your ass to my show. I don't need you on my show. My ratings are higher than yours."

When minimal standards of civility are discarded in favor of such disrespectful speech, is this a reflection or is it a cause of unrestrained expression, and what effect does it have on our leaders and those they are supposed to lead?

CBS BLACKENED ANDY ROONEY'S EYE

"Free expression," it turns out, isn't always free. The Left has its own, ever-changing rule book for determining whose speech should be defended and whose must be silenced.

CBS had its own Marge Schott affair in 1990. Andy Rooney, its popular commentator on the top-rated "60 Minutes," was accused of telling a reporter for a homosexual publication that "blacks have watered down their genes."

In his newspaper column, Rooney wrote that he had been set up by his interviewer because he had indicated his disgust for homosexual practices. "I not only deny the quote, I say the quotation was made up by a young reporter who couldn't take notes," wrote Rooney.

In the past, CBS has resisted efforts by conservative groups to have Dan Rather removed for what they have charged is his blatant leftist and biased reporting. In the Rooney matter, CBS caved in immediately to protests from the Left. One wonders what happened to the First Amendment and the supposed "chilling effect" that comes with censoring speech.

Then–CBS News President David Burke issued a statement in which he said, "I have made it clear that CBS News cannot tolerate such remarks or *anything that approximates such comments* since they in no way reflect the views of this organization." (emphasis mine)

It sounds high-minded, but it is not true.

In 1981, "60 Minutes" reporter Mike Wallace made derogatory comments about blacks and Latinos. As he prepared for a report about the plight of low-income Californians, Wallace was taped by a non-CBS crew talking about the complexity of some sales contracts: "You bet your ass they are hard to read . . . if you're reading them over the watermelon or over the tacos."

Wallace later admitted that reports of his remarks were

"close" to accurate and caught the "flavor" (taco or water-melon?) of what he said. Yet CBS did not dock Wallace a single day's pay, much less suspend him.

The CBS television network seems to have no problem soiling the reputation of another group that is represented in every race, every class, and both genders.

On January 14, 1990, CBS broadcast *Pair of Aces*, a movie that included characters identified as Christians, whose behavior represented anything but traditional Christian principles.

Captain Rip Metcalf, the movie's hero, has an illicit lover named Rose. He also presides and teaches—as if he were a pastor—in a country church, where he tells one man, "Take that damn hat off in church!"

The other so-called "Christian" is Bubba, a teenage football player who is portrayed as a religious fanatic, and who says angels of God told him to murder six girls.

In October 1989, CBS broadcast *Single Women, Married Men*, which it said was "inspired by the actual events in the life of a widely recognized family counselor."

The film opens with alternating scenes of Susan's singing in the church choir and her husband in bed with his lover. The hymn provides the background music for the adulterous bed scene.

Susan's husband leaves her, and after they are divorced, Susan decides to become a therapist and starts a support group for women having affairs with married men.

The rest of the film focuses on the adulteresses as they share in group therapy the sordid details of their lives. One married woman has an affair with a man she meets at church choir practice. When she gets pregnant, she has an abortion.

In its statement about speech that offends blacks and other minorities, CBS takes the high road. But when it comes to stereotyping and ridiculing those who are committed Christians, it's open season and free expression.

WHAT'S WRONG WITH
A LITTLE CENSORSHIP?

I recall debating my good friend Nat Hentoff, the writer and jazz critic, on the First Amendment. Nat is a recognized expert on the subject and an "absolutist" when it comes to free speech. Nat believes that free speech ought to be free and unrestrained, but he acknowledges the classic exceptions, such as crying fire in a crowded theater when there is no fire, libel and slander, and even the right of the U.S. government to prevent the dissemination of its secrets. So, he's not technically an absolutist after all, though it sounds noble.

In debates over free speech, there is a presumption by its defenders that censorship is always, or almost always, bad, and that open expression, no matter what its content or effect, is the highest achievement of a free society.

Not necessarily.

Whenever I debate the issue of censorship, my focus is usually on those who are engaging in "expression" and not the people who are on the receiving end of it.

So-called "artists" who would have been called corrupt or worse two generations ago are today said to be exercising artistic freedom. In some cases, taxpayers are expected to help underwrite this freedom, though if none did these people would have to find honest work, because no one would buy their products on the open market.

A culture defines itself by the limits it sets for its people, much as a football field is defined by its boundaries. If men were angels, no restraints would be needed. But as history proves, men are not angels, not even close, and if they will not be made good, or reasonably acceptable, by a higher power outside of themselves, they must at least be made to conform to a standard that is in the best interest of the culture's preservation and health, as defined by certain objective and immutable standards.

The nation's most direct and forceful experience with censorship came out of the Production Code Administration, established in 1934 not by government, but by the motion picture industry, following public pressure to do something about the perception that movies were going beyond acceptable boundaries.

The code outlined a clear purpose: "No picture shall be produced which will lower the moral standards of those who see it. Hence, the sympathy of the audience should never be thrown to the side of crime, wrongdoing, evil, or sin." The code specified that films were to avoid brutality or sexual promiscuity. It forbade the criticism of any religious group, required proper treatment of the American flag, and outlined appropriate standards for costumes and dance movements.

Implicit in the code was a belief that there was a correlation between pictures and action. It was felt that pictures might give cultural permission to large numbers of people to engage in behavior that was not generally believed to be in the best interest of the nation or to "promote the general welfare."

The code sounds "puritanical" by today's standard of no standards, but it was during this period that Hollywood had its Golden Age, producing films that are today shown on television and occasionally revived in theaters as "classics." The code forbade moviemakers from showing or revealing the techniques of murder in any detail, so the word "arsenic" was struck from many scripts. The depiction of electrocutions was forbidden. Showing childbirth was off-limits, so Scarlett and Melanie were forced to silhouette in *Gone With the Wind*. Mention of prostitution was condemned, so Donna Reed was turned into a bar girl in *From Here to Eternity*. Married couples usually slept in separate beds on-screen.

Sure it denied reality, but movies are not about reality; they're about fantasy and entertainment. Are today's movies "realistic" and reflective of what most people do? In the spring of 1993, the number one box office hit was *Indecent Proposal*, a movie about a man who offers a married woman one million dollars to sleep with him. Most of the debate on radio and TV talk shows ignored the question of adultery and focused instead on the married couple's financial condition. What happened to home equity loans?

The point is not to resurrect every restriction of the movie code. Rather, it is to say that at one time most people realized there was a connection between the artistic expression of a few and the possible emulation of that expression by many.

What are the three big societal problems in contemporary American culture? Are they not the consequences of sex outside of marriage (venereal diseases, abortion, etc.), drug abuse, and violent crime? What are the three main themes of much of the hard-rock music and R-rated films? Are they not sex, drugs, and violence? The public receives cultural permission from the screen to think and act like the actors and actresses they're watching.

What's worse, a little censorship or a lot of social breakdown?

BABY, HAVE A DRINK

Freedom of speech is not absolute. There are serious restrictions on some speech, based on content. Virtually all religious speech or expression (i.e., crèches on public property during Christmas observances) has been banned, particularly if it is in a form that might be regarded as prayer to anything higher than the ceiling or the state.

Civil libertarians have defended the right of authors to express what were once regarded as blasphemies and of public school students to read these expressions (and of teachers to assign them), while simultaneously opposing the use of the Bible or any literature that speaks well of God. This is a kind of discrimination that is more subtle than that which is based on race. In this type of discrimination, the focus is not on the color of one's skin, but on the "color" of one's worldview.

In examining whose speech is to be limited and whose is not, consider a 1991 incident in Seattle in which two restaurant workers were fired after they advised a pregnant customer not to order an alcoholic beverage because they believed alcohol might harm her unborn child.

Twenty-one-year-old Danita Fitch and twenty-two-year-old G. R. Heryford were fired after the pregnant customer became angry and complained to the manager. They had not denied her service. They had only sought to make sure she was fully aware of the medically known facts involving alcohol and unborn babies. Not only were they exercising their freedom of speech, they were fully disclosing, à la cigarette packs, the possible dangers to drinking while pregnant.

Heryford was the first to express himself after the woman ordered a rum daiquiri. He then called for Fitch, who brought with her a beer bottle label cautioning against drinking while pregnant. A sign, which the employees said was placed in an area not likely to be seen by most customers, also warned against alcohol consumption by pregnant women.

New York Times columnist Anna Quindlen was disturbed by such unrestrained expression. While acknowledging that the now former restaurant employees were correct in a medical sense, she wrote that despite the dangers, people ought to be able to do what they want to do, including smoking and tanning their skin, "even when those decisions are wrong."

Quindlen, of course, employs an objective standard for determining what is "wrong," a standard she denies when it comes to the unborn. And, she wrongly equates the dangers in tanning one's own skin or inhaling smoke into one's own lungs with the dangers to which a drinking mother subjects her unborn child. There is a moral difference that Quindlen ignores.

Quindlen calls the ability to make such decisions, even decisions that hurt someone else, "freedom." I call it selfishness when a child is involved. What if the child developed fetal alcohol syndrome? Unlikely, says my doctor, because the woman was nine months pregnant and claimed she had not previously consumed alcohol during her pregnancy. But what if she had? What if she was only four months pregnant when she decided to start drinking alcoholic beverages?

Courts have determined that restaurants and bars can be held legally responsible if customers are involved in automobile accidents and they are found to have blood alcohol levels that exceed legal limits. Why is a written warning on a posted sign or beer bottle considered proper, but a verbal warning from an employee is not?

Suppose the woman had come to the restaurant a month after her baby was born and ordered two drinks, one for herself and one to put in the baby's bottle? Would the waiter have been justified in refusing service to the baby because he or she was underage? Of course. So, what's the difference between protecting a child from alcohol one month after it is born and protecting it a few days before it is born?

The right to do whatever one wishes has achieved cult-like status. Yet what parent instructs a child in the ways of selfishness? What parent tells a child to always put herself first and not to share any cookies or toys with anyone, to look out only for number one? Under the contemporary cultural mandate, when we become adults we are to forget the lessons of selflessness and charity and embark on a life of self-centeredness and self-satisfaction.

The most outrageous examples of "free speech" are winning new legal status and protection in growing numbers, while traditional forms that added something positive to the country are being banned. So, a demonstrator can burn the American flag because this is determined to be a form of "speech," but two restaurant employees, concerned about the health of an unborn child, are to be restricted in sharing the truth, to the point of being fired.

This is a situation that is fueled not by common sense, but by politics, and politics is a terrible basis on which to decide most things.

THE BAND FROM HELL

There are those who contend that violence in music and on film does not influence people to emulate what they see and hear. If that is true, why do advertisers pay so much money (nearly $1 million a minute during the Super Bowl broadcast) in an effort to influence behavior in favor of beer, tires, automobiles, and shaving cream?

Violence and illicit sex, when seen regularly on television and in movies and music, give a type of cultural permission for people to behave as their entertainment role models behave. How could it be otherwise? Bobby-soxers in the forties did not become serial killers after watching Frank Sinatra at the Paramount Theater in New York or listening and dancing to a Glenn Miller tune.

The sixties tore away the veil of decency that had kept entertainment respectable, if not always responsible. As the values and beliefs of a generation were discarded, the new generation needed music and other forms of entertainment that would reflect its increasingly nihilistic worldview.

From the now relatively tame Elvis and the Beatles, we have regressed to the band from Hell, Guns N' Roses, a group for whom perversion would be a step up.

David Geffen, the former president of the label that produced Guns N' Roses' *Use Your Illusion I* and *II*, summed up the catechism of modern entertainment when he said, "When you give the people what they want, they'll show up in droves." A fine, fine epitaph for a generation.

The Guns N' Roses albums are so packed with profanities and vulgaries that the *band* requested a parental advisory label be pasted on the album cover. The warning label could use a warning label. It states, "This album contains language some listeners may find objectionable. They can f—— off and buy something from the New Age section." One album contains a song written by convicted murderer Charles Manson.

It gets worse, as difficult as that may be to comprehend. If there is entertainment for the damned in Hell, Guns N' Roses will be the opening act.

Axl Rose, the foul-mouthed lead "singer," even calls his mother by a sexual epithet that only pornographic magazines and *Rolling Stone* would print. He's the kind of guy you would want your daughter to date, if you were a pervert.

Rolling Stone reviewed the album and saw beyond the band's "thousand points of spite" to a core political message that, we are told, "however indefensible at times, is emblematic of a greater adolescent cancer: an almost total loss of hope compounded by blind, impotent rage and the perverted Reagan-Bush morality in which the actual cloth of the Stars and Stripes is deemed more holy than the freedom and humanity for which it stands."

That's a lot of message for two albums. But the core in this number—indeed, in most numbers these days—is loss of hope, and rage at that loss of hope. Reagan and Bush didn't cause us to lose hope. It was on the way out before they came in. The sixties people promised us paradise. They polluted the paradise we already had and were incapable of building another one in its place.

So many of the children of the children of the sixties barely know their parents. Many of these parents, in numbers disproportionate to those of other generations, are either divorced (sometimes more than once) or work all the time, having little time for meaningful relationships with those they helped to create.

For role models, many have turned to rock stars, who become teachers of the moral code they follow. Just one issue of *Rolling Stone* magazine often contains the concentrated philosophy of a generation, and the poison now infects and affects a second generation. Read Janet Jackson, interviewed on sex (*Rolling Stone*, September 16, 1993), and ask yourself whether she or another black woman—Surgeon General Joycelyn Elders—is likely to have the greater influence.

What is the answer, then? Rampant censorship? No, but labeling records, a practice once advocated by Tipper Gore and Susan Baker through their Parents Music Resource Center, is a good idea. If we can force food manufacturers to label products as to fat and caloric content, why not force the manufacturers of products that cause hardening of the intellectual and spiritual arteries to come clean about the content of their products? This isn't censorship, but the opposite. It would give parents more information about what their kids want to hear and a discussion could ensue that would benefit all concerned.

THE NEW LIMITS TO FREE EXPRESSION

These are supposed to be times of openness to ideas and to each other, no matter what one's political or sexual persuasion. Tolerance is the word the Left wants to see characterize this "modern" generation, yet we see that the least tolerant of all are those who are the chief apostles of tolerance. They want tolerance for what once was widely believed to be perversion, and they wish to censor any thought, speech, or action that does not conform to an agenda designed to remake America in their image.

So, parents who raise legitimate concerns about the content of their children's public school textbooks are quickly labeled trespassers on the holy ground reserved for "academics" and other thought police who are trying to make their children full-fledged members of the Future Secularists of America.

Should gentle persuasion fail to induce parents to bug out of the process of shaping and molding their own children's minds and souls, then the heavy weapons are trotted out. Parents, and their advocates, are quickly denounced with all-purpose pejoratives: "fundamentalists" . . . "bigots" . . . "book burners" . . . "underminer of the First Amendment" . . . "intolerant zealot."

How dare a parent attempt to bar the wonderful masturbatory stories of a Judy Blume, for example, from finding their way into impressionable young minds? Don't parents know that their only job is to give birth to their children and feed and clothe them? Then it is their duty to turn them over to state schools which will tell them that the reason they like bananas on their cereal is because their nearest relative is down at the zoo; that they need condoms in their pockets or purses; that 10 percent of them are homosexual; and that America is no better than any other nation on earth, nor does it embody values and principles that are superior to those of other countries.

Am I trying to have it both ways, arguing for free expression when my values are being censored and defending censorship when those values I disagree with are promoted? I am not. We make exceptions where children are concerned in numerous areas, from driving to drinking alcohol to the ability to sign a contract, even (supposedly) to access to some movies. A child is not considered sufficiently mature to make certain decisions, and society has an obligation to control what goes into a child's body and mind until he or she is old enough to make these decisions. And parents until recently have retained the right to direct their own child's moral development and to see that effort respected, not undermined, by the state.

Seeing that the occasional attacks on parents were not enough to cause them to retreat completely from the playing field, so-called "anticensorship" groups sprung up in the early eighties to stigmatize and ostracize anyone who dared to invade the exclusive territory of the modern education system.

The American Library Association's Office of Intellectual Freedom (a title straight from Orwell's Newspeak dictionary) produced a "Library Bill of Rights," and the American Booksellers Association and Walden Books bought full-page newspaper ads that said, "Censorship cannot eliminate evil. It can only kill freedom."

No matter how much parents protested, they were told that blasphemies, curse words, and stories endorsing sexual permissiveness, anti-Americanism, multiculturalism, and environmentalism were the price all of us must pay to sustain a free society.

What a difference a decade makes!

In the spring of 1991, the *New York Times* responded editorially to a speech on censorship written for President Bush by his top speech writer, Tony Snow, and delivered at the University of Michigan. The president denounced the wave of "political correctness" sweeping the country, including new rules that govern what students may not say and write and what they must read. These rules are designed so as not to offend groups of people the "politically correct" believe need protection from offensive speech. (Whatever happened to the worth of individuals? Why are most people now seen only in terms of the group to which they belong or can be assigned?)

The *Times* defended these rules ("campus speech codes," they came to be called), reasoning that "at some point, speech becomes action—and hateful speech becomes action that a community may protect itself against." If "at some point, speech becomes action," why doesn't the *Times* demand restrictions on some rap groups who call for the sexual and violent abuse of women, the killing of cops, and other antisocial and injurious behavior? The editorial writer's position was that the university's responsibility "is to teach tolerance as well as free speech."

But how can speech be free if it is restricted? Whatever happened to the childhood refrain "Sticks and stones may break my bones, but words will never hurt me"?

The *Times* and much of the education establishment have had a Damascus Road conversion experience on the issue of censorship. In a January 30, 1982, editorial on a Supreme Court case known as "Island Trees," in which the issue was whether a Long Island library could expel books deemed offensive after they reached the shelves, a *Times* editorial said that local governments "may not deny students access to ideas only because they are offensive to the community." The editorial denounced "small groups that have appointed themselves to decontaminate school libraries." It said the motive for yanking books "was to dictate political orthodoxy."

Just what does the newspaper believe is being dictated by the politically correct, if not political orthodoxy? The conservative "demons" of the eighties have been supplanted by new demons in the nineties. The *Times* now says, "The real sources of intolerance on campuses are aggressive racism, sexism, and homophobia," and it sees merit in silencing those who engage in speech that offends racial and sexual minorities and women.

The identical question asked of conservatives in the eighties who were upset by ideas rooted in sexual permissiveness, scatology, and anti-Americanism can now be asked of those who want to force "political correctness" on universities and the rest of the country in the nineties.

The *Times* believes universities can regulate speech so long as such regulation is not "reckless." Who will define what is "reckless" and, to borrow a question from the eighties, why should they be allowed to impose their morality on those who don't agree with them?

The wave of censorship dressed up in the Newspeak sound of "political correctness" is firmly entrenched on many college campuses. Even public television, not noted for showing much that is politically incorrect, could not ignore the level of censorship on many, too many, campuses.

On September 23, 1993, PBS broadcast "Campus Culture Wars: Five Stories about P.C." Among the incidents examined was one at Penn State University where an English professor and feminist thinker was outraged to find a nude painted by Goya hanging in the classroom assigned to her.

Because upset feminists can cause serious harm to a university, a "gender equity specialist" was summoned. In classical "P.C." thinking the gender equity specialist suggested that a painting of a nude male be hung next to the Goya. The feminist professor was not pacified. She said the painting by Goya represented a form of sexual harassment and would have a "chilling effect," so she demanded it be removed.

A student leader of a campus feminist group offered her opinion that "those early paintings" served as a type of pornography because "they didn't have *Playboy* in those days."

Whatever this young woman or her parents are paying for this kind of "education," they are clearly being overcharged.

It is ironic and tragic that liberals who fought against censorship in the eighties now want to engage in their own brand of censorship in the nineties. It is even more pitiful that the closing of the American mind has produced such moronic analysis as that offered by a "feminist" student at Penn State who can't tell the difference between a nude woman in *Playboy* magazine and the classical nudes of Goya's age.

FREE SPEECH AND THE SUPREME COURT

The heavy odor of liberalism that taints the air over our universities these days is enough to disorient many into perpetrating censorship absurdities. Some notable examples:

In 1993, a Jewish student at the University of Pennsylvania faced disciplinary action and possible expulsion for calling a group of black sorority sisters "water buffalo." They were making loud noises outside his dormitory window late at night while he was trying to study. Only an outcry from the *Wall Street Journal* and Rush Limbaugh stopped the persecution against the student.

At the same university, a group of black students confiscated 14,000 copies of the school newspaper because they didn't like some of its content. The same administration that had tried to discipline the Jewish student let the black students off. It would have been politically incorrect to discipline black college students.

In 1991, a Brown University student was expelled when he became drunk and used "hate speech." At about the same time, Stanford University decided that the use of words that offended groups it wanted to protect amounted to "group defamation."

Thankfully, the momentum created by the appointment of more conservative justices to the Supreme Court (which Bill and Hillary Rodham Clinton will now try to reverse) has brought some relief to the aggressiveness of the thought police.

In the spring of 1992, a unanimous Supreme Court struck down so-called "hate crime" laws that many states and cities had passed in an attempt to conform themselves to those who wish to force us to think of people and issues the way they do. The laws imposed special penalties on people who uttered words or behaved in ways that offended certain racial, gender, ethnic, or "sexual orientation" groups. The case involved a St. Paul teenager who had been charged with burning a cross in the backyard of a house owned by a black family.

In the majority opinion, written by Justice Antonin Scalia, the court said the St. Paul ordinance sought to ban expression based on content. "St. Paul," wrote Scalia, "has not singled out an especially offensive mode of expression. It has not, for example, selected for prohibition only those fighting words that communicate ideas in a threatening (as opposed to a merely obnoxious) manner. Rather, it has proscribed fighting words of whatever manner that communicate messages of racial, gender, or religious intolerance, seeking to handicap the expression of particular ideas."

The decision dealt a serious blow to the political correctness movement, which had been moving unchecked across the country, imposing speech codes and "hate crime" laws wherever it went.

LOS ANGELES GETS RELIGION

Nowhere have the forces of intolerance been displayed less tolerantly than in the area of religious speech and practice. It once was believed that a healthy appreciation of God, the Ten Commandments, the Sermon on the Mount, and the Golden Rule were essential building blocks in a child's education and an adult's life.

When he was president of Harvard College, Nathan Pusey observed, "The least that should be expected of a Harvard graduate is that he learn to pronounce the name of God without embarrassment."

The idea that we were made by God, that we had certain responsibilities and an accountability to Him, and that He had established not only a physical order, but a moral order in the universe, was thought for generations to be a concept that was not only good for individuals who would be led to believe such things, but good for nations composed of large numbers of people who shared the same view.

The sixties began to break down that foundation as people rejected the idea of a transcendent God and began a process of creating their own little gods, which they crafted in their image—designer deities, as it were.

This quickly led to an aggressive effort by the Supreme Court and many others to evict God from public schools and, eventually, from public life.

In the nineties, anyone who tries to mention God favorably, particularly on public property or in a public ceremony, is immediately ruled out of order.

Thousands of examples could be used, but one from the now inappropriately named "City of Angels," Los Angeles, will suffice.

In 1991, City Councilman Zev Yaroslavsky called for an official investigation of Assistant Police Chief Robert L. Vernon. His alleged "crime" was that his "conservative Christian beliefs have interfered with his ability to perform official duties fairly and without bias."

Vernon responded with a $10 million lawsuit charging the city with violating his First Amendment rights.

It was not Vernon's job performance that was under attack. No one suggested he had performed his tasks in other than an exemplary manner. What irked Yaroslavsky and other city officials who supported this inquisition was that Vernon spoke openly about his faith in God. Had he been a foulmouthed blasphemer, that would, of course, have been seen as protected speech, but speaking well of God these days can get you in trouble with some people.

What had irked liberal groups in Los Angeles was a speech Vernon gave at his church (on his own time, by the way) in which he spoke against homosexual practices as a sin and advised women to be submissive to their husbands. Both ideas are regarded in some religious circles as traditional beliefs, though not even Vernon's detractors have suggested that he tried to make married women on the police force submit to their husbands.

The chairman of the Police Commission, Stanley Sheinbaum, took the standard liberal view of religion, that it should be closeted: "His private views are his own. But to try to impose his views on his department, where he is an official, then serious questions arise."

They certainly do. To suggest that a person's strongly held religious view is less tolerant than a strongly held antireligious view is morally, intellectually, and politically inconsistent and incorrect.

Robert Vernon was forced out of his job after city officials tarred him as a religious extremist. He lost his $10 million lawsuit against the city. As 1993 ended, Vernon was appealing the judge's decision to dismiss his case without a trial in which witnesses could be called.

Examples of restrictions on religious expression are legion.

Some will recall a "Presidential Biblical Scorecard" published by a conservative religious group during the elections
of 1980, '84, and '88. These were paid for with private funds
and distributed mostly in churches and by direct mail. They
were denounced by liberals as violations of church-state separation and the free exercise of religion. The scorecard
attempted to learn the religious beliefs and political positions
of presidential candidates. The scorecard's authors saw a connection between the two. It then gave what it believed to be
the "correct" religious view on issues.

Editorials and special interest groups who were running
"secular" scorecards of their own denounced the Biblical
Scorecards and suggested they were a threat to the republic.

Rather than celebrate the religious nature of Man, too
many seek to repress it, all in the name of "freedom." I
believe there is a connection between the state's antipathy
toward God and the great social problems that have resulted
from our divorce of Him.

CLEANING UP THE ENVIRONMENT BY TURNING OFF THE TV

The sweetest sound in the world to me these days is the sound made when I push the "off" button on my TV remote control device. If I didn't have to watch television because of my profession as a columnist, I wouldn't. I have found it to be the most banal, empty, and nauseating form of one-way communication on earth (not counting some Washington news conferences).

Each year it seems to get worse, and though the ratings show that the broadcast networks continue to suffer declining audience share, they don't seem to be able to emerge from the sewer, get the message that most of the public has grown weary of their offerings, and give the public something other than subject matter that focuses on the area between the waist and the thigh.

The 1990 season, which ushered in the century's last decade, is as emblematic as any other of how bad things have gotten.

A six-year-old girl opened the season premiere of "Uncle Buck" on CBS with this: "You suck." Later the child explained the crankiness of a female family member this way: "She's ovulating."

Just the kind of "hip talk" adults are supposed to like and aspiring hip kids want to emulate.

CBS entertainment chief Jeff Sagansky told an interviewer he believes kids talk like this in their homes "all over America." He said shows like this are based on "reality." CBS even advertised "Uncle Buck" as a "family show." For the Simpson or Addams families, perhaps.

Actress Sharon Gless, in "The Trials of Rosie O'Neill," revealed to her analyst that she was thinking of surgery for her "tits" and that she wanted to get them "fluffed" (or lifted). This is CBS's world and welcome to it.

On ABC, a woman in the 1990 show "Married People" told her husband, "You're a lying son of a bitch, but I love you." The greeting card companies are bound to inaugurate a new line with such sentiments, since this, too, is supposed to represent reality.

On NBC, "Hull High" featured a female teacher who is hot to trot. She appears in a video production titled *Soft and Round as a Peach.* The executive producer of "Hull High," Gil Grant, said of the sexual innuendo between male students and the gorgeous teacher, "It's a kid fantasy, a boy's fantasy."

That's only a sampling, and more of it can now be seen during the 7–8 P.M. period, once set aside by the Federal Communications Commission as the "family hour," which was supposed to be a sex-free and violence-free, user-friendly entertainment zone.

Incredibly, the networks consistently defend this raunch by saying it is necessary to maintain ratings. But the ratings are in decline because fewer people are watching. Network executives and producers are prisoners of their own ideology. They should get out more—preferably out of Hollywood and New York—and see how real people live and think.

During the 1989–90 season, the number of households watching prime-time television dropped 2 percent from the previous season. The falloff in daytime viewing was even more pronounced: 9 percent overall and 13 percent among women in the network's target group of ages eighteen to forty-nine.

The reason the network and production kingpins don't "get it" was summarized by writer Ben Stein in his book *The View from Sunset Boulevard*: "The super medium of television is spewing out the messages of a few writers and producers (literally in the low hundreds), almost all of whom live in Los Angeles. Television is not necessarily a mirror of anything besides what these few people think. The whole entertainment component of television is dominated by men and women who have a unified, idiosyncratic view of life. When a viewer understands that television is not supposed to be a facsimile of life but instead is what a Hollywood producer thinks life is, the viewer can then understand the match or mismatch between television and what he knows to be true."

The problem is that with culture no longer reflecting even the idea of Truth, the distorted images coming through television and virtually all of the rest of the "media" take on the aura of what truth is.

One way to help restore an intellectual and moral order, at least for the individual, is to turn off the TV and leave it off.

My marriage to television lasted about forty years, since its beginning. With little indication that TV intends to get better, I suspect the divorce will be final, due to irreconcilable differences.

PART THREE

"I WANT TO TAKE YOU HIGHER"

Sly & The Family Stone, Woodstock

CHAPTER 3

The Promise of Pharmaceutical Enlightenment

"Illicit Drug Use Found to Be on Rise among 8th Graders: Responses to Annual Federal Survey Are 'Troublesome'"

That was the headline in an April 14, 1993, *Washington Post* story.

Before the 1960s, news of eighth-graders on drugs would have produced shocked outrage and action. Now, it is only "troublesome." This is the type of laid-back conclusion one might expect from the most drug-overdosed generation in history.

The *Post* story begins with an alarm: "In what some researchers warned could be the start of a worrisome new trend, an annual federally funded survey has found 'significant' increases in the use of marijuana, cocaine, LSD, inhalants, and other illicit substances among eighth-graders, most of whom are thirteen or fourteen years old."

The survey discovered that 11.2 percent of eighth-graders reported trying marijuana in 1992, a one percentage point increase over a similar sample taken in 1991.

The survey also showed that drug use among tenth- and

twelfth-graders had declined, but that seniors were increasingly less likely to view experimentation or even occasional drug use as dangerous. This was said to be an indication that drug use rates for this group might increase in the future.

What Hugh Hefner did for illicit sex, a Harvard professor did for illegal drugs. It was Timothy Leary who urged young people in the sixties to "tune in, turn on, drop out." Many did, and so many reported bad "acid trips" and LSD-induced suicides that the federal government outlawed the substance in 1966. Still, LSD enjoys a significant following. With 8.6 percent of the senior class of 1992 having reported trying it, some drug specialists are warning the drug could make a comeback.

While LSD and cocaine have been the drugs of choice of the more affluent, urban America sometimes prefers to go for the less expensive gusto.

The April 16, 1993, issue of the *New York Times* reported: "Cheap High Lures Youths to Malt Liquor '40s."

The story told of another "Fri-high-day" in the Bronx in which a nineteen-year-old walks into a grocery store and purchases a 40-ounce bottle of Olde English 800 malt liquor. Emerging from the store, he joins his friends and lifts the bottle to his lips like a trumpet and chug-a-lugs the contents.

"It gets you nice," he says.

"It gets you pumped up," says the next boy. "I feel comfortable when I'm drinking a 40."

Malt liquor is essentially beer brewed with sugar, which is what gives it an extra alcoholic kick. The brew is popular among black and Hispanic drinkers. The extra-large-size 40-ounce bottle was introduced in the late 1980s with aggressive marketing campaigns aimed at minorities. In a short period of time it has become the liquid drug of choice for black and Hispanic young people in New York and other American urban areas.

What causes so many young people, who should be excited about life and its possibilities, to drop out of reality so early and descend into the subculture of drug dependency, and often death from overdosing?

The rap group Basehead offers a clue in its song "I Need a Joint": "So how to get over, how to get by? I wish I had a joint to get me high."

"Get over" what? "Get by" what? It can only be despair brought on by lack of hope, meaning, and purpose in life. This is the last will and testament of the sixties generation—a generation that promised these things, but delivered despair, meaninglessness, and life without purpose.

Time magazine reported on the return of the pot culture in a 1993 article called "Hello Again, Mary Jane."

A Seattle band called Supersuckers has a song titled "Tasty Greens," and it's not about spinach.

The title of an album by gangsta rapper Dr. Dre is *The Chronic*, the name of a particularly potent strain of marijuana.

The hard-rock group Living Colour celebrates marijuana in its song "Hemp" this way: "How carefully I've shaped you in the solitude of my days. How peaceful is my mind entwined in cord around my fingers."

Time reports that "marijuana use is also becoming more open among music-industry executives, for whom, according to some, it's replacing 'harder' drugs such as cocaine. Says John Scott of Rush Management, 'I like smoking pot before press interviews, and so do some of the acts. . . . When you have a lot of bands staying in the same hotel, they almost always end up in the same room, smoking."

This behavior and its accompanying values are being drummed, strummed, and sung into the heads of eighth-graders, who are increasingly emulating the behavior of their heroes and idols.

"Troublesome" is an understatement.

THE "WAR" ON DRUGS

If you'd mentioned drugs to me in high school in the late fifties, I would have responded that these were substances one bought at the local pharmacy with an authorized prescription from a doctor. Now the word "drug" is linked in the public mind to illegal substances, crime, and often murder.

Politicians like to fight "wars" on drugs. Unlike other wars, drug wars (and the related "war" on crime) are bipartisan. Politicians—Republicans and Democrats—attempt to outdo each other every election campaign regarding who is "tougher" on crime and who will wage a bigger "war" on drugs. Not much changes, because the attitudes that cause people to turn to drugs have little to do with any penalties the state might impose. Drugs are irrational, and rational approaches to getting people off them, or persuading people not to try them in the first place, are often ineffective, even counterproductive.

Michael and Janet Jackson singing and talking about sex and various rock groups screaming about drugs will always have the ear of the young, who are morally vulnerable and can be easily persuaded to try such things because they are considered "cool." Coolness is the ultimate goal for many of the young. The surgeon general—even a hip-talking one like Dr. Joycelyn Elders—has little chance of penetrating the lifestyle force that surrounds the young. This is not an information gap. This is a generation gap.

The "war" on drugs isn't really a war at all. It is more like a limited police action. The most popular drugs of choice (and the most addictive) are legal. Alcohol and nicotine kill more people every year than all of the other drugs combined.

Young people in the sixties responded to the condemnation they received from adults for trying marijuana, LSD, and other illegal drugs by pointing to their parents' liquor cabinet or refrigerated beer, or the pack of cigarettes in their pockets and purses. Parents argued, "But alcohol and cigarettes are legal. Your drugs are illegal." The argument carried little moral weight. The kids saw drugs as drugs, and they were right.

Campaigns for a "drug-free" America sound nice, but it will never happen. It is a slogan for those who prefer to treat every ailment and disease through the painless process of taking medicine by mouth instead of submitting themselves to radical surgery to stop their spread. As Democratic Senator Patrick Leahy of Vermont has noted about attempts to destroy cocaine labs and disrupt trafficking in South America, "We've spent over a billion dollars down there and we've accomplished virtually nothing."

Information alone is not the key to the drug problem. We have more information about drugs than ever before, yet younger and younger people experiment. Why would anyone want to suck into their lungs the carcinogens in cigarettes, which are the chemical equivalent of bus fumes? As with other drugs, it's the coolness factor. Cigarettes are a sign of independence and rebellion against authority—small comfort to one who develops emphysema, lung cancer, or heart disease.

In his book *Broken Toys, Broken Dreams*, therapist Terry Kellogg writes that drug use has little to do with drugs. "Drug use is about feelings, isolation, hurt, shame, rage, poverty, abuse, greed, etc."

Kellogg notes that the real addiction is not to the drug, but to the high produced by the drug. And why do people want to get high in the first place? "Anything that removes or alters unwanted feelings—anger, pain, fear, sadness, anxiety—can become an addiction." And why would teenagers with so much of their lives ahead of them and seemingly so much to look forward to turn to drugs in such large numbers? It is precisely because they see nothing worth working or living for.

Parents hooked on materialism, twelve-or-more-hour workdays with both parents working (if both are still around), divorce, so little time for family communication and for expressing love and acceptance—these are some of the factors that drive so many young people to cry, "Stop the world, I want to get off." And if they can't get off, they will take something that will make them *feel* as if they were not here.

This is why for so many of the sixties generation, feelings matter more than substance. It is why the president of the United States "feels" our pain. It is why "If It Feels Good, Do It" became an in-your-face rallying cry for the young and the restless.

What was true in the sixties is true today: Drugs are a way for young people to grab power. They can simultaneously escape from a world they hate while punishing parents who have so little time for them.

Remove the purpose for living; remove the meaning of life; teach the Carl Sagan philosophy that the cosmos is all there is or has been; drum into young people that there is no God; hand them condoms and abortion information (and don't be there to catch them when they crack up from the emotional and spiritual damage caused by the relinquishing of adult responsibility to teach the young right from wrong), and what do you have? You have children turning to drugs and sex out of despair, a loss of intimacy, and an anger that boils over against adults who have failed them. Since children have little power, they exercise the only power they do have: They abuse their bodies to get our attention.

An entire generation needs to learn what many were never taught so they can teach their own children what they desperately need to know. As sixties generation member Terry Kellogg puts it, "In having my own children, I realized I was trying to give parenting when I hadn't gotten parenting."

Substance abuse is the number one cause of death among

American teenagers, accounting for more than ten thousand deaths per year. Our kids are crying out for help, for love, for someone to give them a different kind of "high." There is no such thing as "quality time" vs. "quantity time." If it isn't quantity, it can never be quality.

You can't "microwave" children like the dinners that overworked parents cook for their overstressed children. They require time, attention, and heavy doses of love.

WHAT HAPPENED TO THE SUNSHINE?

The most talked-about Broadway show of a generation opened in New York on April 29, 1968, at the Biltmore Theater.

It was called *Hair* and it was more than a musical. It was the artistic incarnation of the values and beliefs of a generation.

Reviewer David Richards summed up its message in a *New York Times* article marking the twenty-fifth anniversary of *Hair*. Richards said the musical brought to Broadway "love beads, polymorphous sex, full-frontal nudity, bare feet, anti–Vietnam War protests, dope, and the conviction that a new world—free, fearless, and unfettered—was dawning.

"It was more than a musical," wrote Richards. "It was a landmark, a litmus test, a temptation, a tourist attraction, an eyeful, a kick. And for a while the country couldn't get enough of it."

Perhaps the most famous song to emerge from the musical (still heard on some "oldies" radio stations) was "The Age of Aquarius." A lyric from the song summed up the youthful idealism that could be found in the smoke-filled marijuana dens and LSD-induced hallucinations: "Harmony and understanding; sympathy and trust abounding." These would be the characteristics of the New World Order According to the Baby Boomers. They would succeed where generations before had failed. Their arrogance was no less offensive because it was nurtured in youth and naïveté.

"Go by the Biltmore on West 47th Street, in fact, vacant since 1988," writes Richards. "It is a shell, decaying a little more each day." As for the stars of the show, "Some died of drugs or AIDS, scourges that *Hair* did not see coming. . . . These days 'flower power' is a florist's slogan, not a generational rallying cry."

The review captures an idealism that at first seemed

enthralling, even compelling, but that quickly turned to despair because it was not founded on a realistic view of humanity or history or the world. The sixties generation thought it could *will* things to be different—despite the evidence of history, despite the obvious flaws in men and women. Those who had been spoiled because they had never been forced to sacrifice didn't understand history, so they were condemned to repeat the mistakes of others.

The promise that came with the drug package was that the enlightenment that would flow from drug use would help those who smoked, or popped, or injected, to escape from a world they hated to one they would love.

Trouble was, they never made it past orbit. They became caught in the gravitational pull of reality, crash-landing on the very planet from which they'd tried to escape.

The double tragedy is that for quite a few of the *Hair* generation, not much has changed, and what they believed then is what they believe today. Many remain addicted to their broken promises and are incapable of repairing their shattered dreams. Michael Butler, who produced *Hair* on Broadway, told the *New York Times*, "What happened with *Hair* is that we discovered flower power wasn't enough to make things happen. And so all these people in the movement went out to get their act together. In that push and drive, we wound up with the Reagan era, which is one of the bad memories of life.

"But the 1990s are going to be very exciting because the people who had mind-altering experiences—and plenty of people did it without grass or LSD—those people never forget the experience. Now those people are in positions of power."

God help us!

CHAPTER 4

The Promise of Sexual Freedom

In the July 1963 issue of *Playboy* magazine, founder and publisher Hugh Hefner wrote that by "associating sex with sin, we have produced a society so guilt-ridden that it is almost impossible to view the subject objectively."

Hefner, a noted theological authority, also asked what kind of God would have man deny his God-given sexual nature. Hefner contended that life is far too complex to restrict sex to marriage and that to suggest that the only purpose of sexual intercourse is to perpetuate the species is to "reduce man to the level of the lower animals."

Now, more than thirty years later, in the age of AIDS and other sexually transmitted diseases, increasing instances of rape and other violent sexual assaults, I wonder what Hefner would say.

Hugh Hefner is the low priest of the sexual revolution. Millions of young men bought his religion of sex as love, without marriage and commitment, and the fiction that it could be indulged in without physical, emotional, and cultural consequences. As men began to believe they could, and should, seek sexual pleasure outside marriage, women at first reacted by participating in this newfound "freedom." More recently, women have begun to experience the pain that comes with disease, unwanted pregnancies, abortions, easy divorce, and the poverty of the greatly diminished lifestyles that often accompany single motherhood, not to mention reduced self-esteem and the feeling that they have been "had."

That God might have been aware of the physical ailments, emotional distress, spiritual consequences, and pain that are caused by sex outside of marriage, and thus wished to spare those He loves from such things by establishing rules of conduct to safeguard us, apparently never occurred to Hefner.

The casualty figures are now in on the sexual revolution, and the body count is staggering.

According to the Alan Guttmacher Institute, a resource for Planned Parenthood that is not known for endorsing what are generally considered to be conservative or traditional values, more than one out of every five Americans are now infected with a viral, sexually transmitted disease. That's 56 million people!

These viral infections, which include herpes and hepatitis B, can be controlled but not cured, and often recur.

The study, published in the spring of 1993, estimated that even more Americans are likely to contract a sexually transmitted disease sometime during their life, and that these diseases would have the greatest effect on women and people under the age of twenty-five.

The Guttmacher report noted that 12 million new sexually transmitted infections occur each year, two-thirds of them to people under twenty-six, and one-fourth to teenagers. The most common are bacterial infections, like gonorrhea or the lesser-known chlamydia (a bacterial infection acquired chiefly through vaginal or anal intercourse), which spread quickly but are treatable with antibiotics.

Because the nation has been preoccupied with AIDS, which affects a much smaller number of people but is 100 percent fatal, these other venereal diseases have received little, if any, publicity in recent years.

The report found women to be disproportionately affected, both because they tend to show fewer symptoms (and thus go untreated for longer periods) and because federal and state programs to combat such diseases tend to be administered in clinics that mainly treat men.

When the current epidemic of venereal diseases began surfacing in the 1970s, some suggested that the only way to avoid these diseases was to not engage in the behavior that put people at risk. They were often mocked and told that such an idea was "unrealistic" because people were going to have sex, no matter what. The emphasis ought to be placed on cures and not on controlling risky behavior, the skeptics claimed.

Now the Guttmacher report has reached the same conclusion: "Given the fact that many of these diseases are viral in nature and can't be cured, the only way to prevent them is to prevent them from occurring in the first place."

Those who have mocked conservatives for three decades for suggesting what were termed "puritanical" and "Victorian" responses to sex are not about to mock the Alan Guttmacher Institute.

The United States now leads the industrialized world in cases of gonorrhea, according to the report. Unmarried people, particularly unmarried teenagers and blacks, are most at risk because these are the groups who tend to have the most sexual partners. But, according to the Guttmacher report, "The general increase in teenage sexual activity puts even teenagers with one partner at increased risk. A recent study in Atlanta found that 24 percent of adolescent women who had only one sexual partner were infected with chlamydia. Symptoms include genital discharge and burning during urination. Women may suffer pain in their lower abdomen or pain during intercourse. Up to three-quarters of cases in women are without symptoms."

It's not a pretty picture, and it certainly isn't a picture Hugh Hefner would include next to his airbrushed *Playboy* models, whose message is that casual, even anonymous, sex continues to be risk-free, all gain and no pain.

Oh, one more statistic that ought to frighten us into monogamy. The Guttmacher report says that about one woman out of nine aged fifteen to forty-four is treated for pelvic inflammatory disease during her reproductive years. "If current trends continue," says the report, "one-half of all women who were fifteen in 1970 will have pelvic inflammatory disease by the year 2000."

Meanwhile, Helen Gurley Brown, the female Hugh Hefner, who has sold women the same lies in her *Cosmopolitan* magazine that Hefner has been selling men in *Playboy,* offers some advice in her latest book, *The Late Show: A Semiwild but Practical Survival Plan for Women over 50.* Brown suggests that older women check out the husbands of other women as potential sexual partners. "Husbands are a source of supply [for sex]," she writes. Regarding the possibility that guilt feelings might arise from an adulterous relationship with another woman's husband, Brown says, "I never feel guilt about the wife, if she can't keep him at home. I'm espousing 'never let sex disappear no matter how old you are.'"

Disease? That doesn't occur on Brown's Fantasy Island.

Unfortunately, the figures don't lie. They show that despite the most massive sex education campaign in history, diseases continue to multiply. Those who suggest such "radical notions" as chastity before marriage and faithfulness in marriage (the essence of such sex education programs as "Sex Respect") are told that these approaches are too puritanical.

The Puritans may have had some problems, but AIDS wasn't one of them.

The surgeon general of the United States, Joycelyn Elders, has chosen to raise the white flag of surrender in two of our most critical cultural battles rather than don a red badge of courage. Dr. Elders thinks that every young girl should keep a condom in her purse when she goes out on a date, and she has proposed (to the consternation and opposition of the White House) that drugs be legalized to take the crime out of them.

Although she didn't say which drugs she thought should be legalized, it seems clear that the health and social consequences of huge numbers of Americans taking all sorts of drugs for any reason seem to have evaded Dr. Elders's attention. At a minimum, she said, such a proposal should be "studied." But President Clinton's response was that he won't even order a study. If drugs had been legal, he said, his brother, Roger, who has struggled with alcoholism, would be dead.

Still, there are those who think wars are won by retreating, not advancing. This, too, is a leftover, failed battle plan from the sixties.

THE MAINSTREAMING OF "ILLEGITIMACY"

Of course, indiscriminate sexual activity can have serious consequences even if disease is avoided. One of the effects of foundational decay has been the rapid rise in out-of-wedlock births.

I detest the word "illegitimate" when it is used to refer to a baby born to people who are not married to each other, almost as much as I dislike the word "bastard" when applied to a child.

The stigma is placed on the wrong person. The baby should not be considered illegitimate, or a bastard, because the child had nothing to do with his or her conception or the circumstances surrounding it.

So, instead of saying that the number of "illegitimate" births in 1990 reached a record high, 1,165,384—the crest of a social tidal wave that began in the sixties—let's say that there were at least 1,165,384 couples who engaged in illegitimate behavior that produced children who deserved better. This doesn't count the 1.6 million abortions that same year, the ultimate in illegitimate behavior.

The 1990 figures (the latest available, although preliminary data for 1991 and 1992 indicate a slight decline in out-of-wedlock births) represent a 75 percent increase over 1980, according to the National Center for Health Statistics. In 1990, 28 percent of all births were to unmarried women; in 1980 this population accounted for 18.4 percent of all births.

PAYING KIDS NOT TO GET PREGNANT

While unrestricted sex has had profound consequences for adults, children have been the greatest victims, as they seek to emulate adults and practice what they are told—in the movies they watch, the music they listen to, and the magazines they read—will bring them happiness and fulfillment.

Despite the clear evidence that sex outside of marriage, particularly among the young, has undermined the family, the country continues to refuse to do what is necessary to restore a moral order.

A Louisiana judge rejected a program that teaches abstinence in the state's public schools because he claimed the idea is religiously based. I wonder what he would think of murder, which was first prohibited in the Ten Commandments.

The chief health officer for Caroline County, Maryland, proposed that teenage girls be paid by the local government not to get pregnant. Dr. John A. Grant said, "I have been watching our pregnancy rates go up for twenty years with a sinking feeling. All the usual things—family planning counseling, adolescent caseworkers—have not been able to budge the rate."

The city of Baltimore in 1987 came up with a crackpot idea to reduce teen pregnancies. The city paid for an ad campaign, including signs on city buses, that asked the question, "What's an Orgy?" It was supposed to encourage discussion between parents and teenagers who saw the ads, so that teenagers might be persuaded to have "safe sex." (Nobody suggests teenagers should be chaste. In addition to being a "religious" view, it is assumed up front that they are going to do it anyway—which then becomes a self-fulfilling prophecy.)

Like all other attempts by state and local governments to reduce the consequences of teen sexual activity, this one didn't work. More than 11 percent of Baltimore girls between fifteen and nineteen become pregnant, the highest rate in Maryland.

The program was doomed from the start, because it doesn't get to the heart of why teenagers engage in sex at ever-earlier ages. The explanation lies less in the physical arena than in the emotional one.

Psychiatrist Walter Byrd of the Minirth-Meier-Byrd Clinic in Arlington, Virginia, tells me, "When families erode and values become relative and not absolute, children must go deeper into their personality hope chests to find something to exchange for affection. They want to connect with the opposite sex at earlier ages, because they see no continuity to life and mostly broken relationships, which include mom and dad."

The *Baltimore Sun*, an editorially liberal newspaper, quoted "officials involved in family planning issues" in Maryland as saying, "No one really knows what will work [in reducing teenage pregnancies], so anything—even paying to entice cooperation—is worth considering."

Nobody knows? Or the editorial writer doesn't know? Surely we know what works. It is obvious. But when our government believes posting the Ten Commandments is an unconstitutional act with greater negative consequences to students who might read them than distributing free condoms from the school nurse's office, then a powerful message has already been sent to young people that no other message from the state will counteract.

The Chesapeake, Virginia, school system has the right idea. Students have been receiving a brochure in their classrooms that seeks to promote chastity as the best means of avoiding the consequences of unmarried sex.

The brochure says, "God has given each person a priceless gift, but many people carelessly give it away." The brochure tells students it is their personal reponsibility to abstain from premarital sex. The American Civil Liberties Union threatened to sue because the brochure mentions God.

Chesapeake School Board Chairman William Spradlin

spoke for most parents when he said, "Isn't it terrible when you attempt to teach what's right and what's wrong and another group takes a stance that you can't tell us what's right and wrong?"

Where did the idea that we can't impose morality come from? It is done all the time—every time a law is passed. We do not shy from attempting to discourage racism, even "homophobia." Aren't such attempts "imposing" a moral view that hating blacks because of their race or homosexuals because of their lifestyle is not good? If we can impose one moral code at this level, why not another? It is because the sex industry (which includes pornographers, abortionists, and condom manufacturers) would go broke if people started behaving responsibly.

We won't teach sexual responsibility, but we lament the consequences of our timidity. Paying girls in Maryland or anywhere else not to get pregnant won't solve their problems or the state's. Giving them something to live for, and the self-esteem that accompanies a purpose in life, will. Hugh Hefner, you have a lot to answer for.

ADULTERY IS GETTING THE BEST OF ME

When marriage vows are trivialized, when adultery is winked at (usually by men, who remain in control of much of the media), this, too, sends an important signal to the culture about what does and does not matter.

Within the recent memory of most of us now alive, a divorced person could not be elected president. Now, an alleged adulterer is president and the American people don't seem to care, so long as these "indiscretions" are not committed publicly.

The question of adultery as it bears on one's integrity and fitness for public office was magnified in the case of Sol Wachtler, chief judge of New York State's highest court.

In Judge Wachtler's case, he was arrested by FBI agents and charged with trying to extort $20,000 from Joy Silverman, a woman with whom he allegedly had a long affair, and threatening to kidnap her daughter. Wachtler confessed to the single felony of threatening to kidnap the girl in a plea-bargain agreement with the government.

Wachtler's close friend, Governor Mario Cuomo, told a news conference, "Even if you assume that everything that Sol's been accused of is true, he was still a good person, who had this narrow telescope aberration. Even if you take this situation at its worst, everything I know about Sol remains true."

This is the moral equivalent of saying that even though John Wilkes Booth did assassinate Abraham Lincoln, he was still a good actor—when in fact the professional abilities of both the actor and the judge are eclipsed by their other deeds.

By praising Wachtler, Governor Cuomo, who often speaks about political matters from a moral point of view, contributed to the rift between personal character and public performance. Dismissing adultery as a "narrow . . . aberration" does an injustice to innocent victims and removes one more "sin" from the dwindling list of biblical commandments we still take seriously.

Can one be "good," as Cuomo asserts, and practice the kind of behavior of which Wachtler was accused and pleaded guilty?

It depends on how you define "good." Webster defines it as "deserving of respect; honorable; something conforming to the moral order of the universe." Wachtler's behavior hardly qualified him for such a description.

In his book *Private Lies*, psychiatrist Frank Pittman addresses the seriousness of adultery: "Infidelity is a breach of the trust, a betrayal of a relationship, a breaking of an agreement."

If a leader will not honor a freely made promise to his wife to forsake all others until death parts them, it is fair to ask on what basis we should expect him to live up to promises and oaths made to the public.

Politicians and media elitists may summarily dismiss the question of adultery as irrelevant, perhaps because so many of them are guilty of practicing it. But it matters a great deal to the general public. Even the most ardent married feminist might care less about her husband's position on women's rights than on where he is spending the night, especially if he is spending it with another woman.

If the governor of New York thinks Wachtler is "good," one might reasonably ask what type of behavior the governor considers bad. When such concepts as adultery come to mean less to the public, we will get a different kind of leadership, lacking that one quality we say we want most: integrity.

THE NEW GAY ARMY

Nowhere has the sixties generation's bequeathing of sexual license been more evident than in the gay rights movement. Though the latest statistics reject earlier inaccurate estimates that 10 percent of the population is homosexual (the Alan Guttmacher Institute received front-page treatment in many newspapers when it released results of a survey that found only 1 percent of men are homosexual), the propaganda war fought by the gay rights lobby has been intense and effective.

The latest battle ground is the nation's military, where fiery arguments have been mounted on both sides regarding gay enlistment.

The continuing flap, which was intensified early on by President Clinton's efforts to pay back a loyal special interest group, is an unnecessary and dangerous attack on what remains of the country's foundational principles. The military is the last public embodiment of traditional morality. If homosexuals succeed in winning approval for their lifestyle (the real goal of this campaign), there will be no stopping them. They will claim that if they can openly fight and die for their country, they should be allowed to legally marry, adopt children, and receive the full approval of the culture.

President Clinton sought to drive a wedge between logic and politics when he argued that people should be judged not on the basis of "who they are," but on "what they do." This presumes that who they are can be separated from what they do, which it cannot.

Most homosexuals have great difficulty controlling the expression of their sexual preference. Dr. Alfred C. Kinsey's 1948 report, which gays like to quote when it comes to the study's inaccurate guess that 10 percent of the country is gay, also said with far more compelling evidence that 28 percent of homosexual males have sex with a thousand or more partners. And 79 percent said half of their sex partners were strangers. In the study, only 1 percent of sexually active homosexual men had fewer than five partners. While the numbers have declined in recent years because of the threat of AIDS and other sexually transmitted diseases, they remain high and far out of proportion to numbers applied to heterosexuals.

The report stated that "little credence can be given to the supposition that homosexual men's 'promiscuity' has been overestimated. . . . Almost half of the white homosexual males said they had at least five hundred different sexual partners during the course of their homosexual careers."

"Careers." An interesting choice of words.

Information like this, focusing on what homosexuals *do* and the risk they pose to themselves and others, ought to be the focal point for debate. But it's not, because that is a debate the gay lobby would lose, so it focuses on other points it thinks it can win.

Nor will this be the end of it, because the gay lobby has a laundry list of demands it wants met, and in President Clinton, homosexuals have an advocate. Large numbers are being hired by the Clinton administration and given important and high-profile positions.

One comment by the president is especially revealing. He told a news conference, early in his term, "Our country is changing, and we have to listen to other points of view." This is not leadership by conviction and the pursuit of objective truth. This is "followership" by public opinion poll using a cultural barometer. A nation whose leadership does only what seems expedient and not what is right is destined for the dustbin of history, no matter what its military power or economic strength.

RAPING THE AMERICAN MIND

Even more alarming than the sixties' legacy of sexual permissiveness is its legacy of sexual violence.

Civil libertarians criticize those who try to establish a link between depictions of sexual activity in film or music and real-life sexual activity, especially when it is suggested that violence associated with sex might cause some people to emulate such acts on real people. Serial killer Ted Bundy said pornography made him kill, but assorted "experts" said that wasn't possible and that Bundy was trying to con us.

Not possible that words and images can influence behavior? If that's true, why do advertisers spend millions of dollars to sell their products on television?

For an explanation as to why women are raped in record numbers—as many as 1,871 per day, according to one rape victims' group—one need only check out MTV. A Michael Jackson video called "In the Closet" shows Michael and a woman making pelvic thrusts at each other. Michael sings, "There's something about you, baby, that makes me want to give it to you." He's not talking about a wrapped birthday gift. This is the same Michael Jackson his supporters defended against allegations that he had molested young boys. "He's so innocent," many said. Sure, like Madonna is innocent.

The day I tuned in, the Jackson video was immediately followed by that of another "artist," whose offering was called "Baby's Got Back." In this one, women shake their behinds at the camera, various fruits and vegetables shaped like body parts are shown, and the rapper says he likes women's buttocks and feels like "sticking it" to them.

Pornography is worse, but this stuff is the entry-level material for those who will go deeper into depravity, even all the way to rape and violence against women.

Feminist and antipornography crusader Andrea Dworkin wrote the *New York Times* about her own sexual abuse. She believes rape is linked to the tolerance and promotion of pornography and sexual images that tell men it is okay to treat women badly.

Dworkin wrote, "Freedom looks different when you are the one it is being practiced on. Those sexy expletives are the hate words he uses on you while he is using you." Dworkin added that men "act out pornography. They have acted it out on me."

She correctly indicts men who use the First Amendment as their shield so they may traffic for profit in the misery of women. "They eroticize inequality in a way that materially promotes rape, battery, maiming, and bondage; they make a product they know dehumanizes, degrades, and exploits women; they hurt women to make pornography, and the consumers use the pornography in assaults both verbal and physical."

There have been suggestions by some members of Congress that legislation is needed that would compensate victims of sexual assault if that assault can be linked to pornography. So far no bill has passed, and much of the media establishment has lobbied heavily against any such measure.

Yet, it may be the least a society can do to protect women from sexual predators.

One wonders what Hugh Hefner's reaction would be if his wife or daughter were raped and the perpetrator were found to have a closetful of *Playboy* magazines that he said excited him enough to assault women.

CANADIAN SUN SETS ON PORNOGRAPHY

Canadian authorities see more clearly than Americans the connection between pornography and behavior, and they have done something about it.

The Canadian Supreme Court ruled in 1992 that pornography can cause violence against women. Canadian criminal law provides that any publication that has as a "dominant characteristic" the "undue exploitation of sex" is obscene. (However, the law does not cover private possession of obscene material, and the penalty for retailers is usually a fine.)

The Canadian court found that the right of women to be protected from men who would cause them harm is greater than the right of these same men to purchase pornography: "The proliferation of materials which seriously offend the values fundamental to our society is a substantial concern which justifies restricting the otherwise full exercise of the freedom of expression."

The court found something that apparently has eluded American legal jurisprudence: a causal relationship between the depiction of sexual exploitation of women and children in publications and films, and the victimization of these groups.

That there *is* a connection between pornography and violence should seem obvious, given the evidence of recent studies.

A 1991 study by the Los Angeles Police Department showed that pornography was used in two-thirds of the child molestation cases over a ten-year period. The police department in Louisville, Kentucky, reached a similar conclusion in 1984.

Researchers Murray Straus and Larry Baron found in a 1983 University of New Hampshire study that Alaska and Nevada have two things in common: They lead all states in pornography use per capita, and they have more incidents of rape than any other state. Straus and Baron also found "an unusually high correlation" in all states between sex magazine readership and the rape rate. They said, "The fact that sex magazine readership is strongly and consistently correlated with rape supports the theory that porn endorses attitudes that increase the likelihood of rape."

American civil libertarians cannot have it both ways. Rape, child molestation, and sexual harassment continue to be problems. If liberals care about women and other victims of sex crimes, they should favor the conclusions of the Canadian Supreme Court.

PART FOUR

"SOUL SACRIFICE"

Santana, Woodstock

CHAPTER 5

The Promise
of God's Death

"God Is Dead," announced *Time* magazine in its April 8, 1966, cover story.

God was no longer relevant to this new generation, which would do its own creating, perform its own miracles, and write its own commandments—which would not be etched in stone, but written in a more fluid substance so they could be changed at any time.

In short, this generation had replaced God—indeed, it had become God—so the only logical course of action was to declare the real God (while not admitting that He/She ever existed) dead.

Trouble is, it became difficult to live as if there were no God. Appeals to standards fall flat if there is no standard-giver. Higher things such as love and faith and virtue have nothing to hold them up and they quickly crash with the culture if there is no supreme Authority, no personal deity to give them (and us) meaning, purpose, and direction.

While the nation now grapples with a huge budget deficit, it gives scant attention to a growing cultural, social, spiritual, and moral deficit.

Democratic Senator Daniel Patrick Moynihan, one of the few leaders to consistently speak of the consequences of a social deficit, wrote an article for the January 1993 issue of *American Scholar* titled "Defining Deviancy Down." Its thesis was that

America is undergoing a profound social crisis and that the nation has more or less decided to pretend it isn't happening.

Moynihan uses the psychologist's word "denial" to describe the many backs that have been turned toward this cultural deviancy. From crime to welfare to drugs to deteriorating schools—the evidence abounds. What does not abound is an admission of the problem and the commitment necessary to do something about it. The greatest resistance comes from those who continue to seek solutions in government programs.

There is a refusal to consider that while the problem is in each of us, the answer lies outside—indeed above—all of us, and the way to treat afflictions of the heart and soul is not with placebos of this world.

Peggy Noonan, the former speech writer for Ronald Reagan and George Bush, correctly diagnosed the nation's spiritual crisis in the September 14, 1992, issue of *Forbes* magazine.

Noonan recalled the poet W. H. Auden, who labeled his era the "age of anxiety." In her opinion, what was at the heart of the dread in those days, just a few years into the modern era, was the realization that "we were beginning to lose God—banishing him from the scene, from our consciousness, losing the assumption that he was part of the daily drama, or its maker.

"And it is a terrible thing when people lose God. Life is difficult and people are afraid, and to be without God is to lose man's great source of consolation and coherence. There is a phrase I once heard or made up that I think of when I think about what people with deep faith must get from God: the love that assuages all."

How did we reach such a point that a nation founded in part on presumptions of God's existence would then deny that existence and any accountability to Him? Was it accidental or was it deliberate? Rather than God "dying," did the culture commit homicide (or suicide)?

Noonan accurately observes, "Somewhere in the seventies, or the sixties, we started expecting to be happy, and changed our lives (left town, left families, switched jobs) if we were not. And society strained and cracked in the storm.

"I think we have lost the old knowledge that happiness is overrated—that, in a way, life is overrated. We have lost, somehow, a sense of mystery—about us, our purpose, our meaning, our role. Our ancestors believed in two worlds, and understood this to be the solitary, poor, nasty, brutish, and short one. We are the first generations of man that actually expected to find happiness here on earth, and our search for it has caused such—unhappiness.

"The reason: If you do not believe in another, higher world, if you believe only in the flat material world around you, if you believe this is your only chance at happiness—if that is what you believe, then you are not disappointed when the world does not give you a good measure of its riches, you are despairing."

Despair amidst an endless search for significance. It is the station at which the sixties generation has, for the most part, arrived. They seem always to be seeking, but never able to find, a knowledge of the truth.

Science rejoiced when God's "death" was proclaimed. Science has been trying to replace God for centuries. But what is science if God is dead?

Philip Johnson, professor of law at Boalt Hall, the law school of the University of California at Berkeley, asked that question in an article he wrote for the May 10, 1993, issue of the *Wall Street Journal.*

"Once theology was the queen of the sciences," Johnson began. "Lately it has been replaced by physics, but there are signs that the physicists want to become theologians. . . . Ambitions like this have important consequences."

Indeed they do.

In discussing a number of new books that seek to use science to disprove God, Johnson draws on one by Nobel Prize–winning physicist Steven Weinberg, who promotes a philosophy of reductionism which, says Johnson, asserts that consciousness is a product of brain chemistry, that life processes are directed by the DNA genetic program, that the DNA code itself is reducible to the laws governing the physics and chemistry of lifeless matter, and that everything is ultimately traceable to the initial conditions of the Big Bang.

Johnson says Weinberg hopes "that discovery of a unified particle theory will convince the public that nature is governed by impersonal laws, and thus discredit 'traditional beliefs,'" which range from relatively harmless superstitions like astrology to 'ideologies of the most vicious sort.' He does not say explicitly what vicious ideologies he has in mind . . . but he leaves careful readers little doubt. The 'dark forces of religious enthusiasm' are gathering strength in Asia and Africa, he warns, and reason and tolerance are not safe even in the West. Reductionist science must come to the rescue of rationality, supplanting religious visions with a cheerless prospect of an impersonal universe that exists for no purpose."

It's a real "downer," as a sixties-generation person might cynically put it. Science will prove once and for all that God isn't dead; He never existed. And this will be such a "blessing" (if that word is to ever again be tolerated) that humanity will celebrate its existence in an impersonal, materialistic, survival-of-the-fittest, directionless, purposeless universe with no life after death and no place other than the cosmos.

For this we are supposed to be profoundly grateful? For this we should cry out in lamentations.

Concludes Philip Johnson, "Naturalistic metaphysics relegates questions like how we should live or what we should value to the realm of subjective opinion. It provides no sacred common ground, other than a supposedly value-free science, to unite differing human groups and give them a foundation to reason from."

Science and theology have functioned best when they are properly aligned, not at each other's throats or seeking to replace the other. When scientists such as Newton and Galileo saw a world order created by God, they viewed science as a means to explain a small part of what God had made. Modern (and not a few ancient) scientists and some theologians seek to dethrone God and make science God.

Science does not even consider that a God who can be explained would not be God. Can a refrigerator explain how it was made? Then why should we expect a human to explain or understand all of the intricacies of the universe?

This is not a theological tract that seeks to prove God, but the consequences—political, social, and personal—to a society that declares God dead or irrelevant are profound. One does not have to accept God in one's personal life or to order that life according to every principle of Scripture to enjoy full civil and human rights in this world, but it is difficult to argue in favor of a culture that forgets God, given ancient and modern history. From Moses to Abraham Lincoln to Aleksandr Solzhenitsyn have come warnings of severe consequences to nations that forget God. The proof that they were right is found in the carcasses of long-dead cultures and philosophies that are strewn along the road of history.

No matter how many discoveries science makes (and as a Jewish guide who was only marginally religious once told me in Israel, "Science has never disproved the Bible and has frequently had to reconsider conclusions in light of archaeological discoveries"), science has no power to touch the heart and soul of Man. It cannot transform a sinner into a saint. It is incapable of influencing the spirit of Man, no matter how much it may want to. There is a considerable amount of evidence—some of it scientific—involved in matters of faith, but there comes a point where individuals must decide that science doesn't have all the answers and, based on facts as they understand them, take a reasonable step of faith based on considerable evidence and accept the rest of scriptural truth grounded not on the logic of Man, but on the character and nature of God.

Like others of his generation, President Clinton is uncomfortable with what the secularists have done to the national landscape by their expunging of religious faith. He has read Stephen L. Carter's book *The Culture of Disbelief* and has quoted from it several times at public and private meetings.

Carter writes, "My concern . . . is with the question of what religiously devout people should do when they confront state policies that require them to act counter to what they believe is the will of God, or to acquiesce in conduct by others that they believe God forbids. The intuition of our contemporary political or legal culture is that they should do nothing. . . .

"The intuition says, in short, that religion is like building model airplanes, just another hobby. . . . This intuition, then, is one that in the end must destroy either religion or the ideal of liberal democracy. That is a prospect that can please only those who hate one or the other or both."

Actually, as the Founders well knew, religious faith sustains liberal democracy because it provides a base for beliefs that undergird the highest ideals and aspirations of humankind. This is why the subject cannot be viewed as a "hobby" or a diversion, or, especially, as irrelevant to the political and cultural debate.

Is a theocracy the answer to our social and cultural decline? Absolutely not. But a proper understanding of the nature of Man, the purpose of government, and the relationship of both to a God who created government to control the base nature of Man *is* the answer. The unraveling of nations occurs when Man attempts to topple God and replace His authority with our own. We then come to believe the government is our keeper and that therefore we shall not want. This is what is at the heart of the Clinton administration's social policies, especially universal health care.

The decline of American culture, hastened by spiritual deficiency, continues unabated in the nineties. But the infection began in the sixties, and those who caught it continue to afflict the rest of us.

IF NOT GOD, WHO?
IF NOT ABSOLUTES, WHAT?

"The danger when men stop believing in God," said G. K. Chesterton, "is not that they will believe in nothing, but that they will believe in anything." This summarizes the point at which our modern culture has arrived.

Issues and ideas are no longer debated with the objective of separating truth from falsehood. Opinion polls have replaced the Ten Commandments as our standard. The only "sin" left in America is the presumption that truth can be found, or worse, that you have found it. All questions remain open and unresolved except those that the elite have determined are closed and which they themselves resolved. The television networks and most print journalists refuse to grant legitimacy to any other view except the prevailing one. So they trash those views with which they disagree (if they condescend to consider them at all) and promote the views with which they agree, often unfairly and in an imbalanced manner, presenting fiction as truth and error as doctrinal purity.

The consequences for a culture that has deadened its senses to God can be seen almost daily. Sometimes the contrast is quite stark, as it was with the most watched congressional confirmation hearing in history.

When the Senate Judiciary Committee considered the nomination of Clarence Thomas for the Supreme Court, a debate was rekindled over the origin of law. In his testimony, Thomas appealed to what the Founders referred to as "natural law," which they always mentioned in the context of a revealed "heavenly" law, as they assumed most people regarded it.

A Harvard Law School professor, Laurence Tribe, reflected the arrogance of most modernists about everything that predates the television age when he wrote concerning Clarence

Thomas that he "is the first Supreme Court nominee in fifty years to maintain that natural law should be readily consulted in constitutional interpretation."

A question for Tribe would be why he thinks legal interpretations by judges of the past fifty years should be regarded as superior to those of the previous 150 years or, indeed, superior to those of the Founders, or of those who preceded and influenced them.

No idea can be isolated from other ideas. There is a flow to history. When considering "natural law," the history of the idea must be examined.

As constitutional attorney John Whitehead has defined it in his book *The Second American Revolution*, natural law "posits that there is a form of higher law in nature, which man's reason can discover."

The natural-law concept originated among the ancient Greeks. While many interpret natural law in different ways, it was Aristotle who shaped the way most came to view it in Europe and thus in the modern era. Aristotle distinguished between natural law and "man-made" laws. In his view, laws made by people might be good or bad, depending upon whether they conformed to a set of absolute laws that were to be found in nature. It was society's obligation to organize itself to live in a utopian state where the natural laws could be exercised.

Plato, who some called the first "totalitarian philosopher," thought it part of natural law that the state would serve as the highest authority over man. In the ideal society as defined by Plato, children were to be taken away from parents at birth and reared by the state. As John Whitehead writes, "Plato drew the presuppositional blueprint for a Communist society, all in the name of natural law."

Thomas Aquinas (who tried to integrate Christian theology's concept of man's fallen nature with Aristotelian philosophy) and Jean-Jacques Rousseau (who saw natural law as an expression of the general will) were among many throughout history who have sought to define and direct the concept of natural law.

Today, Laurence Tribe and his legal fellow travelers want us to view natural law as being in a state of flux and in need of regular updating so as to conform to the wishes of the people, forgetting about what preceded the last fifty years.

When Thomas Jefferson wrote of "the laws of nature and of nature's God," he drew on a phrase that was often quoted by the Founders. They had read *Commentaries on the Laws of England* by jurist William Blackstone, whose work was widely studied in American law schools until about fifty years ago (it is more than a coincidence that things changed after Blackstone was no longer read).

Blackstone viewed natural law as having a source: "This will of his Maker is called the law of Nature. For as God, when he created matter, and endued it with a principle of mobility, established certain rules for the perpetual direction of that motion; so, when he created Man, and endued him with free will to conduct himself in all parts of life, he laid down certain immutable laws of human nature. . . . These are eternal, immutable laws of good and evil."

Having given credit to God as the source of natural law and showing how he endowed rights which then became unalienable, as Jefferson later acknowledged, Blackstone reached this conclusion about such a law: "This law of nature being coeval with mankind, and dictated by God himself, is of course superior in obligation to any other. It is binding over all the globe, in all countries and at all times. *No human laws are of any validity if contrary to this;* and such of them as are valid derive all their force and all of their authority, mediately or immediately, from this original." (emphasis mine)

These are the roads that diverge at the crossroads of two philosophies, one that begins with the law and mind of an infinite Creator-God, and one that begins and remains in the mind of fallen Man. Not only is this the great debate in law, it is the great debate of history. Is man autonomous and free to do what he wishes, or is he created by God for a purpose and answerable to God for his life?

All other questions are eternally irrelevant if the right answers are not given to these questions.

THE TORCH AND THE LIGHT

On election night 1992, Vice President-elect Al Gore exuded in his victory speech, "We are the children of the modern age."

The torch had been passed to a new generation, but this statement was symbolic of the power failure that has caused the light to go out on the social and moral questions that are critical to any nation.

Who are these "children," and have they grown up or do they remain childlike and idealistically immature inside their adult bodies? What have they given us?

They and the value system they forced on America have given us condoms in the schools, not self-control and virtue; "recreational" drugs, not a "high" that comes from honor, duty, and character; no-fault divorce, not commitment and a determination to work things out no matter how one feels; prenuptial agreements and a nuclear strike on the family; AIDS and low-quality television that increasingly focuses on the region between the waist and the thigh, rarely visiting the things of the mind and spirit.

So many liberals have dismissed all but the most impersonal religion and the power of spiritual ideas from the center of public life.

In an often-ignored line from his Inaugural Address in January 1961, President John F. Kennedy said, "The rights of man come not from the generosity of the state but from the hand of God." Kennedy called us "heirs of that first great revolution" and spoke of allies who shared our "cultural and spiritual origins."

Kennedy didn't believe in taxing and spending as a solution to America's problems. He said to "those people in the huts and villages of half the globe struggling to break the bonds of mass misery, we pledge our best efforts to help them help themselves."

This was a practical application of the biblical principle that "if a man will not work, neither shall he eat."

Kennedy's address was full of references to what Americans can and must do for themselves. Government would be a helper, but not a keeper.

"In your hands, my fellow citizens, more than mine," Kennedy said, "will rest the final success or failure of our course."

In his most famous admonition, Kennedy said, "And so, my fellow Americans: Ask not what your country can do for you—ask what you can do for your country. My fellow citizens of the world: Ask not what America can do for you, but what together we can do for the freedom of man."

Modern Democrats, who seem to have made Faust-like bargains with every special interest devil in America, would never nominate a person who said such things today. They have disconnected from such ideals and now label as "intolerant" and "fundamentalists" and "bigots" those who presume a higher authority, a higher purpose to life than the supremacy of the state.

Theologian Carl Henry, in his book *Twilight of a Great Civilization*, has succinctly summarized the tension between those who are prisoners of modern times and those who have freed themselves from these times and are likely to emerge and be seen by future generations as men and women of character and virtue: "The real heroes of our time are those who in a faithless age hold, live, and share their faith in God. Genuine revolutionary courage belongs to those who remain true to God even if atheistic rulers force them underground or punish citizens simply for being Christians.

"The true immortals will be those who seek to apply the principles of the Bible concretely to the complicated realities of modern life, who preserve a devout and virtuous family life, who are faithful to the abiding values of yesterday, today, and tomorrow."

THE REPUBLICANS AND THEIR MESSAGE

The Republican party, after suffering its first defeat in a national election in twelve years, is flirting with abandoning the social and cultural agenda that had previously energized enough Americans to produce margins of victory in 1968, '72, '80, '84, and '88.

If the GOP demotes this agenda from its previous position of importance, Republicans will guarantee themselves permanent minority status and the deserved ridicule of the future. Before administering a Dr. Jack Kevorkian–like suicidal remedy, the GOP would do well to look to its founder.

On March 6, 1860, presidential candidate Abraham Lincoln gave a campaign speech in New Haven, Connecticut, on the great moral issue of his time: slavery. As reported by the *Daily Republican* newspaper, Lincoln said, "What we want, and all we want, is to have with us the men who think slavery is wrong. [How can you say you] hate slavery, and are opposed to it, but yet act with the Democratic party? . . . You say that you think slavery is wrong, but you denounce all attempts to restrain it. Is there anything else that you think is wrong, that you are not willing to deal with as wrong? Why are you so careful, so tender of this one and no other? You will not let us do a single thing as if it was wrong! We must not call it wrong in the Slave States because it is there; we must not call it wrong in politics because that is bringing morality into politics; and we must not call it wrong in the pulpit because that is bringing politics into religion."

Replace the word "slavery" with the word "abortion," read Lincoln's remarks again, and we have the debate within the modern Republican party, whose new chairman, Haley Barbour, has said, "If we make abortion a test of being a Republican, we need our heads examined."

Modern Republicans are said to lack a message. What they lack is conviction of the kind that created their party on a foundation of moral principles. Too many modern Republicans suffer from poor leadership. Too many blow an uncertain trumpet and play from different sets of sheet music. The disarray in the GOP is caused by a reluctance of too many of its members to know and speak the truth and to call wrong the things that are wrong.

Former GOP Chairman Rich Bond warned against clinging to "zealotry masquerading as principle." He should have warned against the greater danger of cowardice disguised as conviction, of running away from issues simply because they are difficult. Avoiding tough choices cannot and should not earn the respect, the trust, or the votes of a majority of the people.

There is only one thing worse than convictions that are never applied. It is those that are never held. A valueless life is a terrible waste.

Republicans didn't lose the White House in 1992 because they were too zealous. They lost it because it appeared that President Bush had no principles, at least none for which he was willing to fight. Accommodation sounds well-mannered, but too often it is a cover-up for vacillation and appeasement.

Irving Kristol contributed this warning in the February 1, 1993, *Wall Street Journal*: "The Democrats are never going to be able to welcome the religious, but if the Republicans keep them at arm's length instead of embracing them, and shaping their political thinking, a third party and a restructuring of American politics are certain. One way or another, in the decades ahead, they will not be denied."

OUT WITH THE OLD, IN WITH THE NEW

Not too long ago, when people graduated from high school with the ability to read and write and to tell right from wrong according to a generally accepted standard, most people thought it a good idea to shield children from baser things, such as foul language, sex before marriage, and life without God.

Now that we have "progressed" into the computer age, we consider ourselves more intelligent. We now feel it essential that the baser things should be considered normal and an essential part of a child's education and that the nobler things, such as a God concept, are to be placed where the baser things once were: outside the immediate consciousness of students.

So, the Supreme Court, misinterpreting the First Amendment (as it has done since 1947), rules that the states are prohibited from mentioning God favorably. (Unfavorable references are said to be protected by the same First Amendment that forbids favorable references.)

The outrageous became the ludicrous following a 1992 ruling by the Supreme Court called *Lee* v. *Weisman*. A rabbi was invited to deliver a graduation invocation and benediction at a Rhode Island public high school. The prayer was so generic, God might not have recognized it as having been directed at Him! Nevertheless, a student and a parent were offended, and that was all that was necessary for the ever-vigilant God police to move in and arrest the thinking of students, whose minds are not supposed to wander higher than the ceiling unless it is toward Carl Sagan's cosmos.

The Court ruled that neither rabbis nor anyone else could be invited by a school for the specific purpose of offering a prayer, no matter how innocuous and without theological content it might be.

The ludicrous soon followed.

Afraid of what the Court *might* do, the superintendent of Frederick County, Virginia, schools, Thomas Malcolm, issued a memorandum that was viewed by many who read it as a prohibition against the use of the words "Christmas" and "Easter." Fearing a lawsuit (which no one had threatened to file), Malcolm said words such as "winter holiday" might be substituted for Christmas and "spring break" for Easter. Parties could be held during these seasons, but they should be referred to as "holiday parties." All employees of the school district were to heed the memorandum.

When threatened with a lawsuit from the Rutherford Institute, a legal organization that argues religious freedom cases in court, Malcolm withheld implementing the policy until a committee he created could further study the matter.

What about the rights of most people who still refer to these "holidays" by their traditional names? They are expected to lay down their rights and allow the minority to trample on them without protest.

The irony is that Virginia is a state with mandatory sex education, beginning in kindergarten. Five-year-olds are to learn about AIDS and to be prepared for the introduction of condoms later in elementary school. They are to be told that homosexuality is one of many lifestyles that are okay, but they are to be denied hearing about anything that might remind them of God. The words—*the words*—"Christmas" and "Easter" are thought to be a bigger threat to children in public school than some of the words associated with sex education?

How many people, besides the Virgin Mary, ever got pregnant from a direct encounter with God?

The American government once was viewed as a protector and defender, even a reflector, of religious tradition and thinking. It has become an enemy of people with religious faith who think that faith ought not to be locked by the state behind the church and synagogue doors.

With the help of pressure groups, government now has

crossed over into the final frontier of bigotry, what writer and Catholic theologian Michael Novak calls "Christophobia." Traditional Christians and Jews are the new counterculture—aliens in a land their forefathers' beliefs and values established and built. Anything that seems to come from or lead to a world not of this one is deemed offensive, illegal, and unwise.

What amazes is that a *school superintendent* would issue a memo discouraging traditional values, evoking memories of the way the former Soviet Union once required Christmas and other religious holidays to be observed in that country. Soviet government mandates also forbade the use of the word "Christmas," requiring "winter holiday" for the season and "Father Frost" as the Christ substitute. Decorated trees were to be referred to as "New Year's trees."

Now, the new Russia has opened its doors not only to Christmas and Easter, but to the faith the Soviet Union tried so hard to exterminate. Russian educators have met with American religious leaders and educators. They are bringing teachers and Bibles into their public schools and restoring the values and ethical base they see their children as having lost during seven decades of official atheism.

America, which once promoted God and biblical values, now opposes them, and Russia, which once opposed God and biblical values, now welcomes and promotes them. Having been without religious freedom and having experienced persecution for most of this century, Russians are awakening to the value of what they lost. This country, having been established on a foundation of religious values and expression, now flirts with paganism, unaware of what it is like to live in a nation where faith is persecuted by one's own government.

Nadiia Hundert knows what it's like. In 1989, she wrote a letter to the publication *Soviet Ukraine*. Hundert's message ought to be read in Virginia and wherever religious intolerance is practiced.

"Today, as a consequence of an atheistic upbringing," she

wrote, "we are knee-deep in alcoholics, drug addicts, other chemically dependent individuals, loafers, bums, criminals, savages, uncouths, dullards, cruel and frightful juveniles who commit crimes for the fun of it. These are people who were brought up by nonbeliever parents and an atheistic society. Christians lived with religion for a thousand years and provided us with a rich heritage, which we have succeeded in destroying without fire or flood. . . . It would be a very good thing if, in restructuring the school curriculum, the education specialists included teaching of religion in our schools."

It appears the Russians learned something from us. It also appears we learned nothing from them.

GOD: THE COMEBACK

Though religious intolerance is a pervasive part of public life, there *are* signs that the idea of God is making a resurgence.

The upsurge in spiritual interest, especially the so-called "New Age" movement in which many sixties flower children have found permission to explore their inner selves without having to acknowledge the existence of a personal God who might require something from them and want to do something for them, again affirms the third part of the three-part human condition: body-mind-spirit.

Time magazine came full circle from its 1966 "God Is Dead" cover story when it published an April 1993 cover on "The Generation That Forgot God." The article chronicled the generation that forgot or rejected God and how many of its members are now searching for "designer churches" that will give them what they're looking for. Some are even going much deeper in their quest for spiritual truth.

Among the letters to the editor that appeared two weeks after the cover story was one from R. Steven Chambers of Salt Lake City: "As a Baby Boomer, I am fascinated by my generation's apparent return to religion. Unfortunately, it seems that the philosophy of the Me generation has carried over to the quest for spiritual wealth. We appear to be searching not for a moral code, but for a justification of our lifestyle. While it is true that Jesus never turned people away for asking too many questions, there is no mention in the New Testament of packaging the answers to meet the wishes of the audiences or to fill the pews, and no one said the way to heaven was easy."

(The Rev.) Leisa M. Richards, a twenty-nine-year-old United Methodist minister from Salmon, Idaho, wrote *Time* and reflected a more judgmental view of the generation that forgot God: "I have come to believe what a church official once told me: The major problem facing the church today is the attitude that it is here to serve the individual—not the other way around. Most people are shopping for a God who will meet their needs. They will sacrifice nothing, especially themselves."

There are severe problems for individuals and nations that forget God. Individuals are cheated of a real sense of purpose, beyond taking up space on the planet and contributing to the landfill. Nations that have forgotten or opposed God are condemned to focus only on economics as the highest good ("The economy, stupid" became the mantra of the Clinton campaign). They become little more than ratifiers of the self-interest of their citizens.

PART FIVE

"WITH A LITTLE HELP FROM MY FRIENDS"

Joe Cocker, Woodstock

CHAPTER 6

The Promise
to End Poverty

The biblical promise that "the poor you will always have with you" was not meant to assume a permanent and unchanging underclass. Nor was the sixties generation's promise of a "safety net for all" meant to provide a hammock for an entire segment of society. At one time I was poor, which is to say my income was low. I might have qualified for food stamps, had they been available in the early sixties. Once I even received unemployment checks for a few weeks when I was out of work. But I never thought of my low income as a permanent condition. I had desire, incentive, and drive. And America gave me opportunity, which is all anyone can (or should) ask for. I did the rest. I was determined to succeed.

Liberal "reformers" tell today's poor that something other than their attitude, lifestyle choices, and lack of determination will always keep them poor and it is only the welfare state and the poverty industry that sustains their existence and keeps them alive.

For those poor who happen to be black (and most poor people are white), racism is usually the explanation offered by big government and too many poor black people for their miserable condition.

The fact that many blacks have made it into the middle class and that a growing number are counted among the upper class is never used to encourage other blacks to make the decisions their more successful brothers and sisters have made. Successful blacks are the exception, the poor are told. White people hate you. You can't do it alone. You need us, the "civil rights establishment." It has become a self-fulfilling prophecy that has bred a permanent underclass dependent on government.

Every election cycle, and after a riot or racial incident, politicians and journalists play the now-familiar game of "Pin the Blame for Poverty on Someone." If a Republican is in the White House, they play "Pin the Tail on the Elephant." The donkey never gets pinned.

Typical of the familiar response to poverty was the reaction by the former chairman of the U.S. Civil Rights Commission, Arthur Fletcher, after the 1992 Los Angeles riots. Fletcher called for a "massive" federal effort (the word "small" is not in your average government official's vocabulary) to confront racial division, poverty, and urban problems.

We've already had a massive federal effort. It has cost taxpayers nearly $4 trillion over the last thirty years. We fought the war on poverty. The poor and the taxpayers who footed the bill lost.

Hearing Arthur Fletcher's call for a second war on poverty, then-President Bush—echoing his vice president, Dan Quayle—correctly responded that the Los Angeles riots were "not about civil rights" or "the great issues of equality" or even poverty, but "the brutality of the mob, pure and simple." If poverty was the cause of the riots, every poor person should have rioted. But most poor people did not riot, did not loot, and did not beat whites with their fists and throw bricks at the head of truck driver Reginald Denny.

That these riots were anything but spontaneous and not rooted in poverty was evident from comments in a telephone conversation I had with Rev. E. V. Hill, pastor of Mt. Zion Missionary Baptist Church in south-central Los Angeles, where the trouble started. Hill told me the rioters were "filling their pantries and living rooms and replacing old furniture. Every drugstore was targeted professionally, because drugs are there. Jewelry stores, too. It was an organized pattern in the Watts riot in the sixties, and the same was true this time."

Hill noted that the law-abiding, many of them poor, protested the state jury verdict acquitting the officers in the Rodney King beating by praying, singing, and speaking. These and the poor blacks who risked their lives by rescuing the wounded and injured from the streets are the real heroes and role models. But the press, especially television, chose to promote the other image, along with the prescription of more and costlier government, which has not worked, and cannot work.

These incidents are used by politicians who seek the vote, but not the welfare of the poor, to stampede the country into new rounds of spending on programs that have failed. The fact is, no federal program can approach the impact on crime and other forms of antisocial behavior that the return of the black man as husband to his wife and father to his children would have (and this is also true of the white man who has abandoned his family and left his wife and children in depleted financial condition).

Fortunately, some fresh black faces and new black voices are beginning to say the same thing, but much of the press still prefers to listen to the guilt and grievance victims squad led by the NAACP, Jesse Jackson, and Rep. John Conyers, who has proposed that the federal government pay reparations to every black American because of slavery.

Since 1965, the number of out-of-wedlock births has more than tripled. It is now a cliché that more young black men are part of the criminal justice system (in prison, on probation, or paroled) than are in college.

New York University professor Lawrence Mead says, "What matters for success is less whether your father was rich or poor than whether you knew your father at all." There is no substitute for—and nothing as effective as—a man who keeps his promises to his wife and family and loves his children.

A study published in the *Journal of Research in Crime and Delinquency* found that the proportion of single-parent households in a community predicts its rates of violent crime and burglary.

The proper response by the federal government to urban crime should be to revise and reform its poverty policies, including tax laws, which undermine family stability and cohesiveness. Wisconsin is one state that has taken the lead with divorce and welfare reform. Other states would do well to follow.

KILLING HIM SOFTLY WITH HIS SONG

In Washington, D.C., which has been America's murder capital more often than any other city, shootings frequently dominate the local news, sometimes consuming as much as ten minutes of a newscast. Because there are so many shootings and homicides, it takes a creative killer to capture more than fleeting public attention.

One such case involved a nineteen-year-old boy who shot and killed a newlywed woman in a drive-by shooting. "I just felt like killing somebody," the boy-man explained.

It was not the "greed" of the eighties that created such deranged juveniles. It was the refusal of the culture to impose (yes, impose) a set of standards rooted in immutable values on young people, who will not on their own grow up to do things that promote the general welfare.

Listened to the music of their lives lately? Watched MTV? Seen any of the R-rated films that are so full of cultural permission to curse and to engage in violence and sex? These messages have replaced reading, writing, math and, yes, religion, as the center of life.

Criminals aren't born, they are made, and America is manufacturing them in record numbers, causing prisons to overflow. Many who should be in prison never go, or are quickly released because of lack of space. Still, "experts" are blind to the truth. One of the prophets of the modern view of poverty, crime, and criminals is former Attorney General Ramsey Clark. "The basic solution for most crime is economic—homes, health, education, employment, beauty," says Clark. "If the law is to be enforced—and rights fulfilled for the poor—we must end poverty. Until we do, there will be no equal protection of the laws. To permit conditions that breed antisocial conduct to continue is our greatest crime."

This is what might be called the "humanitarian" view of crime. As Stephen Sondheim wrote in *West Side Story*, these people "are depraved on account of they're deprived." If true, every "deprived" person should act out their resulting depravity. But they don't.

More than seventy years before Ramsey Clark, criminologist Enrico Ferri wrote, "If you regard the general condition of misery as the sole cause of criminality, then you cannot get around the difficulty that out of the thousand individuals living in misery from the day of their birth to that of their death, only one hundred to two hundred become criminals. . . . If poverty were the sole determining cause, a thousand out of a thousand poor ought to become criminals. If only two hundred become criminals, then poverty alone is not sufficient to explain criminality."

WHERE IS POVERTY'S HUMAN FACE?

Who or what causes poverty? Sometimes it seems an unanswerable question in an unwinnable debate. Conservatives fault the welfare state and the programs of Lyndon Johnson's Great Society. Liberals say it's the fault of the Reagan and Bush years, which sought to undermine programs they claim were working.

It should be pointed out that some people are poor, and will remain so, because they lack motivation and vision. Nothing can be done for them. Others are poor but are highly motivated and view poverty as a conquerable condition. Some enjoy the support of intact families, a key ingredient for emancipation from poverty because one then has others with whom he can share his success and from whom he can draw encouragement, sustenance, even assistance. Such persons will need little or no outside help.

Lastly, there are the poor who might emerge from poverty if they had access to a ladder. Their motivation may be dormant only because they have not been shown a way out, but it could be revived if they were offered hope.

It is this last group that needs and deserves national and individual attention. But this group needs something far better than government handouts. It needs improved self-esteem, the primary motivating force in any life.

But self-esteem does not come by others telling you that you're okay. Instead, it rises out of a set of core values and beliefs. That's what the phrase "virtue is its own reward," coined by our grandparents' generation, meant. Virtue and virtuous living produce self-esteem. You feel better about yourself when you are doing good. If people believe they have value they are more likely to dream and work than if they think they are worthless.

A major reason for the persistence of poverty is that the poor are largely faceless. Television gives us "spokespeople" for the poor, who are usually rich because they make money from the poverty industry. Most Americans are generous and would willingly assist someone less fortunate than themselves if they saw the person as motivated and honest.

One solution to much of the poverty problem (we'll never get rid of it entirely) might lie in America's most powerful medium: television. Why couldn't networks and local stations produce public-service announcements (they could be called "a moment of hope")? Needy people—who have been screened to weed out the frauds—would tell their personal stories to their fellow citizens.

A fund could be set up that would meet the short-term needs of the poor. If they needed money for education or job training, or for child care while they pursued these goals, it would be provided. The objective would be to liberate the poor from poverty and poverty programs. Fund administrators would hold beneficiaries accountable.

People could contribute $10 or $20 a month to individuals or families to whom they have been assigned. Spare-change receptacles at convenience stores would allow all to contribute and to feel they were truly doing something positive to help those in real need.

Some contributors (those who pledged $20 in monthly giving) could be matched with a poor person locally. Government's role would be supportive, not primary.

As more people stepped in to help the poor and more poor people no longer needed government assistance, the government would renovate its crumbling financial foundation. AFDC (Aid to Families with Dependent Children) grants would be capped and eventually reduced (this is what is happening in Wisconsin) so that the system would no longer reward irresponsible behavior by those who have successive children out of wedlock and apply for greater welfare payments because they know they will be subsidized in making the wrong lifestyle choices and decisions.

What can government do to shore up the family, the

basic foundational building block of any culture? One thing it can do is to return to the attitude it once had about divorce, which was not too long ago something far more difficult to obtain than it is today. People seeking driver's licenses must take tests, and many of them take lessons to learn to drive responsibly. If stable families are in the country's interest, what would be wrong with requiring people to seek counseling before they receive their state marriage license, and counseling before being granted a divorce?

At a minimum, the "no-fault" divorce, an invention of the no-responsibility sixties generation, should be eliminated, especially for those couples with young children, except in documented cases of physical or extreme mental abuse.

Some believe there are too many poor people to be helped. The question is not how many poor there are, but how many better-off people there are who would be willing to offer meaningful assistance. We won't know that until we try some innovative approaches to personalize poverty, and to personalize solutions.

THE POVERTY WAR: MANY SMALL BATTLES

One of the groups (are there any individuals left anymore?) seeking to address the nagging poverty problem in America is called The Communitarians. This group, made up of liberals, neoconservatives and political in-betweens, argues that parents are the biggest weapon against poverty. The group's members also believe that political discussion should focus less on rights and entitlements and more on obligations and responsibilities.

The Communitarians (and this sounds too simple to be true, but it is) think parents should make a new commitment to their children. Instead of focusing on "making it" and acquiring mountains of material things, The Communitarians suggest, parents should come home from work earlier and recognize their primary duty to their children and their fellow citizens.

I recall an exchange I once had on Phil Donahue's show. Phil said to me, "The trouble with you conservatives is that you have such simple answers to complex problems." I replied, "The trouble with you liberals, Phil, is that you've ignored the simple answers and that's why the problems have become complex."

The Communitarians think it is a good idea to do something about reducing the rate of divorce, which has clearly worked against the interests of children, society, and even the splitting adults.

Increasing the deduction for dependent children would serve as an economic stimulus for most families, including those that would like for one of its two working parents to be able to stay home with young children.

Sixty-two percent of American families are now headed by single mothers, compared to just 28 percent in 1959. The absent father (and fathers can be absent by working too much as well as by having abandoned the family) is the single largest factor contributing to poverty. Nearly all contemporary welfare programs subsidize this kind of family and penalize with high taxes and other disincentives those who want to work their way off the welfare list.

A WAR ON BLACKS

Some white liberals are too cautious and sophisticated to admit it now, but when *Roe* v. *Wade* was decided and the unborn lost in 1973, a few were heard to say that they expected abortion on demand to help end the welfare problem, by which they meant it would hold down the black population, which they regarded as being largely dependent on government aid.

Jesse Jackson, before he caught a case of political pragmatism, denounced *Roe* as "black genocide." Others said it was tailor-made for whites' "ghetto problem"; these racists believed abortion would suppress the illegitimate birth rate among blacks and thus reduce welfare spending.

Because abortion on demand did not eliminate or reduce poverty as some had hoped, the new ghetto-blaster is Norplant, a drug that is surgically inserted into a woman's arm and is supposed to keep her from getting pregnant for up to five years.

The *Philadelphia Inquirer* editorialized in December 1990 that Norplant was a good idea that should be tried. In case potential candidates did not share the newspaper's enthusiasm, the editorialist suggested, the incentive could be sweetened with a check. Women would be paid to try it.

Black employees at the newspaper rebelled over the editorial, as did many black readers. But why should they? Is not Norplant just the next logical step down into the cultural pit? From aborting babies, to removing feeding tubes from "hopeless" cases, to Dr. Jack Kevorkian and his euthanasia machine, we have already crossed a number of ethical bridges and then set them aflame so it will be difficult to return.

The emotional responses of some of the *Inquirer*'s staff were revealing.

Vanessa Williams, an *Inquirer* reporter and president of the local chapter of the Association of Black Journalists, wrote a letter calling the editorial "a tacit endorsement of slow genocide" and "a short step between extortion and coercion."

Garry Howard, an assistant sports editor at the *Inquirer,* recounted how he grew up in the South Bronx as one of six children born to a welfare mother. He won a full scholarship to an elite preschool, and eventually worked his way out of the ghetto. "According to that idea [paying welfare mothers to take contraceptives], a person like me wouldn't be here, wouldn't have the chance to be an exception. Without exceptions, there is no hope."

That argument alone takes care of about 90 percent of the contentions made by advocates of abortion on demand, most of which are rooted in economics or matters of "convenience."

We are not yet at the point where we are forcing contraceptives on welfare mothers, but we are close. As soon as society decides it is in the interest of those with more money and power to force contraceptives or sterilization on the poor because new lives they might produce would be a "burden" to society, a very important bridge, indeed, will have been crossed and burned for good.

If all this sounds vaguely familiar, it should. In an address to the Prussian Council on Health on July 2, 1932, a Dr. Schopohl warned that "the biological heritage of the German people is menaced" because families with "an unsound heritage are increasingly unchecked."

It was this attitude toward human life that led to the destruction not only of the German handicapped, but ultimately of the unwanted unborn of Eastern Europe and the Jews. A report issued in 1943 noted that the Reich decree pertaining to "interruptions of pregnancy" was considered "a safety measure for the German people" because the "high birthrate of female Eastern [European] workers and female Poles represented a biological weapon against the German people."

According to a letter addressed to the Reich Commissioner for the Strengthening of Germanism, the designation "undesirable population increase" provided the basis for forcing abortions on workers at Auschwitz.

Norplant is our modern "final solution," and the answer, for some, to the "poverty problem."

THE "POVERTY PENTAGON"

Robert Woodson is a black veteran of the civil rights movement of the sixties who has defected to the "other side."

Woodson founded the National Center for Neighborhood Enterprise, which seeks to deploy the resources of the private sector to solve neighborhood problems.

While acknowledging the evils of racism, Woodson doesn't dwell on them. Instead he directs his fire at a poverty "industry" that he says benefits from keeping people poor.

Of the welfare industry, Woodson has written, "What we have built in the name of the poor is a Poverty Pentagon. And in this huge conglomerate of programs for the poor, the principal beneficiaries are not the poor but those who make their living from the poor. We have, in many cases, programs that do not improve the conditions of the poor but actually exacerbate the very problems they were designed to solve."

Selections from Woodson's thinking are contained in *Challenging the Civil Rights Establishment: Profiles of a New Black Vanguard,* by Joseph G. Contin and Brad Stetson. The book gives underquoted or never-interviewed black academics and social leaders a chance to present their views.

Woodson's thinking about racism and poverty began to change when he was in the army: "After two years of running to bars and running around while in the army, I stopped and said, 'I'm not going to be like a lot of black people who say white people got their foot on my neck. The way not to become a part of that is to prepare yourself.' I turned some of that energy and anger into achievement."

Woodson adds that he didn't fight for integration; he fought against segregation: "[The civil rights establishment's] embrace of integration and busing really turned me off. Also I didn't like their embrace of the poverty program . . . when I knew it was ripping people off. . . . They seemed to be impressed with issues that were important to middle- or upper-income blacks, but did little for lower-income blacks."

Woodson has a message the establishment doesn't want to hear, because if it is heard, accepted, and acted on, the poor will have jobs and the establishment will be out of work: "Power does not come from what someone concedes. It is in controlling your own behavior. At the street level, people are less concerned about racism, than they are getting to the store, past drug dealers."

The number one problem in America, Woodson believes, is not racism, but the breakup and breakdown of the family, particularly the black family (a point made elsewhere in this book but which cannot be repeated enough, given the repetition in our culture of other explanations and excuses).

As late as 1959, 78 percent of all black families were intact and less than 2 percent of black children were reared in households in which the mother was not married. This was before civil rights legislation, before the Voting Rights Act, and before the war on poverty. Blacks were still being lynched in the South, but black families were mostly together and provided a strength for their children that is no longer there.

When the black family began to break up, the troubles started. Government attempted to become black children's surrogate parent and the surrogate husband to black women.

We need to listen less to the voices of Jesse Jackson and the leadership of the NAACP. We need to hear black voices that the major media have silenced because they often do not conform to the message of the civil rights establishment.

We would do well to consider great thinkers like the educator Booker T. Washington, who said, "Time, patience, and constant achievement are great factors in the rise of a race"; or like Maxine Hankins Caine, who wrote in *Destiny* magazine, "Our leaders will boycott for jobs and money, but not for decency"; or like Shelby Steele: "For every white I have met who is a racist, I have met twenty more who have seen me as an equal."

And we should realize that poverty is not a black or white issue, but an economic situation that many of the poor can change on their own by making right decisions, and that others can be helped to overcome through means that will eventually allow them to become self-sustaining.

CHAPTER 7

The Promise of Preferential Treatment for the Young and the Strong

HEALTH CARE HAZARDS TO OUR HEALTH

When I was growing up, a doctor was thought to be one who did all he or she could to preserve and enhance life. Now the medical profession has crossed the divide into practices that can take life. From abortion to infanticide to euthanasia, medicine seems increasingly on the side of those who would make life "cost-effective" or "qualitative" according to new standards that bioethicists are developing for bureaucrats whose chief concerns are cost and not the inalienable right to life of an individual.

The Clinton administration's plan to nationalize health care and create perhaps the biggest government bureaucracy of all time ensures that the power over our health—as well as the life-and-death decisions that go with that power—will increasingly be exercised by government, which will be less and less accountable to any standard except the bottom line and the next election.

Abortion, infanticide, and euthanasia will become, under socialized medicine, means to achieving "better health for all" as the value of life is eclipsed by the "quality of life."

When human life ceases to be unique and is seen only as part of an evolutionary cycle with no beginning and no purpose, then it requires little imagination to predict the eventual establishment of "qualitarian life centers" where government employees will determine, according to a formula that is written by and for the young and healthy, that the old and sickly ought not to live because they only "burden" everyone else. At that point the view of older Americans as obsolete, which had its start in the sixties, will have achieved a frightening literalness.

Former Colorado Governor Richard Lamm has become an advocate of euthanasia for the elderly. He would (and has) bristled at such a description, but when the niceties and polite and bureaucratic language are stripped away, that is the essence of what he supports.

Lamm now directs the Center for Public Policy and Contemporary Issues at the University of Denver. He (like Hillary Rodham Clinton and her health care task force) has seized on a problem that concerns most Americans: the growing cost of health care and the difficulty many have in accessing it. But Lamm takes this legitimate concern and offers a sixties-type solution that appeals to a growing number of people who value some lives less than others.

As with all horrors, the arguments for euthanasia ride on the backs of the most extreme cases: ninety-year-olds who have lived full lives and who now suffer terminal ailments, and are kept alive only by expensive equipment and technology that is draining the resources (and inheritance) of the elderly person's loved ones; or the severely retarded (of special interest to me because my brother is somewhat retarded) who would be "better off dead," according to the diagnosis of those who think themselves qualified to judge who should live and who should die—and when. It is almost as if a new constitutional right has been created: the right to be free of burdens that impede our ability to make money, have fun, and consume stuff.

Yet, one of my favorite lines from *The Fantasticks*, a wonderful off-Broadway musical that, ironically, ushered in the sixties, suggests that society has missed the point: "Deep in December, it's nice to remember, without a hurt, the heart is hollow." (No, the decade wasn't a total failure.) The fact is, burdenless lives create superficial people whose only interest is themselves. How pathetic would be a world filled with such people, yet we are on the way to creating exactly that.

In an environment and in a nation that celebrates life, the "hard cases" can be dealt with humanely and with compassion. What we must *not* do is treat the "inconvenient"— whether it be the elderly, the disabled, or the retarded—as "broken" people, as less than human, because they will then be viewed as disposable, like soiled diapers or throwaway bottles and cans.

Lamm believes "there is a fundamental tension between the health of an individual and the health of a society." His concern is that we shouldn't spend too much to save the life of an elderly person, when, if we allow that person to die, more money will be available to treat younger people.

Coming from a man who once said, "The elderly have a duty to die," such a view of society's balance sheet is not likely to win nods of acceptance from those approaching their "golden years."

I have heard some people compare the elderly to leaves that fall from trees in the fall, forming compost heaps. Greeting card makers might find it a little difficult to sell messages that refer to aging mom and dad as compost heaps or fertilizer, but if there is a market for them we can be sure they will be on the card racks soon, printed on environmentally correct recycled paper.

The danger in Lamm's philosophy is that he speaks of

cost before worth; of bottom lines before the value of the individual; of pragmatism before sanctity.

The medical profession was built on a foundation and a philosophy that viewed human beings as unique and above all other categories of living things. Even the Hippocratic Oath, formulated in ancient Greece, recognized the uniqueness of human life and regarded the medical profession as a kind of priesthood to administer the sacraments of medicine in a manner designed to preserve and improve lives.

Those for whom cost becomes paramount propose a new medical world order based not on the worth of Man as made in the image of God (which is all that separates Man from plants and animals), but on a utilitarian standard. Access to such a system will always consider the bottom line.

Any reformation of health care must begin with the proper philosophical view of Man. Otherwise, medical science and technology replace God—indeed, they become God, deciding who should live and who should die, and when. In her attempt to "reform" health care, Hillary Rodham Clinton said that we must define when human life begins and when it ends. When historic (even biblical) and traditional medical definitions of such things are abandoned and government begins to consider such definitions its job, we are all potentially at risk if we belong to a category that falls out of favor with the authoritarian elite.

With a flawed view of Man, doctors, medical technocrats, and government authorities will decide life-and-death issues like ancient Caesars in the Roman Coliseum by turning thumbs up or down. Without a proper respect for human life as having innate dignity and worth, plug-pulling on ninety-year-olds will quickly develop into active euthanasia (as it has in the Netherlands) for those who fail to meet an arbitrary standard based on cost. Those deemed "unfit" or "unwanted" under this new equation will be quickly jettisoned like spent booster rockets when they are seen to be a strain on the federal budget or on families who don't want to give up an hour or two on Sunday afternoon to visit granny in the rest home, or to spend any of their inheritance on keeping her alive.

When medicine regards cost as paramount in determining the value of a life, those things that once were unthinkable become thinkable, even probable. Former Surgeon General C. Everett Koop has said, "When a hospital is geared to save lives at any cost, this attitude affects health care down to the most mundane level. On the other hand, when one set of patients can be eliminated at will, the whole spirit of struggling to save lives is lost, and it is not long before a doctor or nurse will say, 'Why try so hard on anybody? After all, we deliberately fail to treat some patients and we kill others.' Even if it were not expressed this blatantly, an erosion takes place, which over a number of years would undermine the care of all patients in any institution that kills any patient in its care."

Medicine has heroically and traditionally been a guardian for the weak, the elderly, the infirm, the young, and the unborn. Now, legislators will soon be confronted with the question of whether those protections should be maintained by force of law or removed by force of economic "realities." Such a step would reduce the ethical and moral questions of medicine to the level of export-import quotas.

Without an abiding belief in the sanctity of all human life, the materialistic-humanistic views expressed by Nobel laureate Francis Crick in 1978 seem less extreme: "No newborn infant should be declared human until it has passed certain tests regarding its genetic endowment, and if it fails these tests it forfeits the right to live."

It is a very short step from there to declaring other lives null and void when they fail totally arbitrary tests established by "professionals."

It is the difference between seeing your aging parents as unique human beings and viewing them as potential bags of fertilizer for society's lawn.

A LICENSE TO KILL

James Bond had a license to kill from the British government. That was fiction by Ian Fleming.

In reality, the Dutch government, which ought to know better because of its experience with the occupying Nazis, has licensed its doctors to kill. The conditions set down by the Dutch parliament under which physicians may literally kill their patients are supposedly "strict," but an important line has been erased for medicine and for patients that will not be easily redrawn.

The purpose of the now rarely taken Hippocratic Oath was to give voice to a revulsion against the utilitarian motives behind abortion, infanticide, and euthanasia in ancient Greece. Now that abortion is legal, it is rarely taken and, when it is, the abortion prohibition is usually ignored.

The Oath established for the first time "a complete separation between killing and curing," in the words of the late anthropologist Margaret Mead. The Oath, which was pagan in its origin, would later be strengthened by the ethical and moral principles contained in the Old and New Testaments.

But the sixties generation decided for all of us that these principles, even those with pagan origins, were no longer relevant to a modern age, and so we are rapidly reverting to pre-Hippocrates times, in which technique, skill, and outcome, rather than intrinsic value, are to guide physicians as they determine who should live and who should die.

In his book *The New Medicine*, Nigel M. DeS. Cameron writes, "The real question is this: Is medicine essentially a matter of medical technique? Or is it, rather, a matter of values, of moral commitments in the exercise of clinical skills?" These are not tangential questions. They are central to health care and to the value a society places on life in any generation and in any nation.

The Dutch passed their euthanasia law precisely because,

as Cameron warns: "The medical profession has simply forgotten to reflect on the nature of the medical enterprise. It
has no single governing concept of what it is doing. A fatal
combination of technological advance and ethical flux has led
to the progressive disintegration of the idea of medicine." In
fact, most medical schools today take only a peripheral interest in "bioethics."

If the Author of life becomes anonymous, if the reason
for curing becomes utilitarian and economic, we cease viewing Man as a unique creature endowed with certain inalienable rights. We then begin to believe that much of medicine
is worthless sentimentality and that we can, and should, save
gobs of money by denying all but the "fit" and mentally
gifted access to medical care and restoration to good health.

This should sound familiar to anyone not so overdosed
on television that the closest they get to history is the instant
replay. This was precisely the view of Man held by much of
the German medical profession under the Nazis. German
doctors forged an unholy alliance with Hitler and became his
willing servants in a hellish attempt to exterminate the Jewish
people and other "unwanteds" in pursuit of the "master
race." Contemporaries of mine don't like to be reminded of
what the Nazis did, saying it is an extreme example. But all
extremes begin with small compromises that lead inevitably,
when unchecked, to the gas chambers and ovens.

Once doctors engage in killing to satisfy state objectives,
as the Nazi experience showed us, there will be no limits
placed on the use of their "skills." Then, as Dr. Karl Gunning, former president of the League of Dutch Physicians,
believes, an irreversible slide begins. "Our society is moving
very quickly from birth control to death control," Gunning
has warned.

Shame on the Dutch people for allowing such a thing to
happen. Are there no history books in The Hague?

Parliamentarians should have read Benno Muller-Hill's
book *Murderous Science*, in which the professor of genetics at

the University of Cologne focuses on the transformation of medicine before and during the war years.

Muller-Hill quotes a letter from Hitler: "Reichsleiter Buhler and Dr. Brandt are specially designated physicians, such that patients who are judged incurable after the most thorough review of their condition which is possible can be granted mercy killing."

Notice the language. At the death camps there were no "thorough reviews," and the killing was anything but a "mercy" to those who were killed and their families. People were exterminated when they failed to live up to the arbitrary standard established by Hitler for the master race.

There is no moral difference between what Hitler did then and what the Dutch parliament has now done (and what some Americans are proposing be done). Empowering Dutch physicians with the right to kill is a dangerous precedent that the Dutch people will regret, but by then it will be too late. The "die" has been cast.

HBO THINKS IT BETTER NOT TO BE BORN

There is a new philosophy making the rounds that says because of high crime, drugs, violence, and so many other social maladies, there are societal benefits (and benefits to the unborn child) to be derived from abortion. According to this philosophy, by killing so many of the unborn we are preventing future criminals and assorted weirdos from entering the human family. Under this view, killing can have positive benefits for society. Ken Auletta of the *New York Daily News* and Barbara Reynolds of *USA Today* (a black woman who should be more sensitive to where such ideas lead) have spoken favorably of this view.

Hollywood, which remains socially, morally, and intellectually disconnected from reality and most of the nation, often gives voice to such views. Few better (or worse) examples could be found than in a 1992 made-for-television HBO special called *A Private Matter.*

The story was about Sherri Finkbine, who was "Miss Sherri" on an old television show called "Romper Room," back when children were taught right from wrong and people understood there were definitions of such things.

Finkbine and her husband, Bob, a high school teacher, had four children. When she became pregnant with her fifth child, she took a drug that Bob had bought for her in London that was supposed to help her sleep. The drug was thalidomide. It was soon discovered to cause severe defects to the unborn child when a woman took it during pregnancy.

When Finkbine's doctor told her the baby was likely to be born deformed, she and Bob opted for an abortion. Trouble is, abortion was not legal in most states at the time, so the Finkbines went to Sweden (a nation that imposes penalties when parents spank their born children) for the procedure.

The film tried to take the moral high road by showing

the "agony" involved in the Finkbines' decision. This has always puzzled me. If the unborn child is not human—indeed, if he or she is just barely connected tissue (sonograms now reveal a small human)—then why agonize at all? This must be a matter of conditioning that the behaviorists will squeeze out of us over time.

The film also subtly suggested that the handicapped are enormous burdens that "normal people" ought not be required to bear. Viewers might also have concluded that handicapped children and adults would consider it a favor if their parents had aborted them, because they are doomed to lives of misery and unfulfilled dreams.

Too bad HBO didn't also show a film called *Whatever Happened to the Human Race?* In 1978, when the film was made, every network and most local stations (the ABC affiliate in Washington, D.C., was an exception) had refused to air it, despite the offer by its producers to pay for the time.

The film featured the late philosopher Francis Schaeffer and Dr. C. Everett Koop. In it, former patients of Koop are interviewed by him. They were born with maladies that are now considered "legitimate" reasons for abortion. All were helped by surgery Koop performed when he was chief of pediatric surgery at Philadelphia Children's Hospital.

One woman told Koop, "You don't realize how it will turn out when you start. Now I'm a normal, functioning human being. . . . Because the start was a little abnormal, it doesn't mean you're going to finish that way."

Another patient said, "I'm very glad to be alive. I live a full, meaningful life. I have many friends and many things I want to do in life."

A young man named Craig, whose mother took thalidomide, was born with no arms below the elbow and with impaired, but usable, legs. He graduated from Cal Poly with a degree in philosophy and from Covenant Theological Seminary. Craig said of those who wish to abort or euthanize the handicapped, "They don't understand. They're talking about people. They only see the handicap. When I was born, my dad said, 'This one needs our love more.' People make a mistake when they look at the handicap, not the person."

The voices of these and millions of other handicapped people are silenced because they remind us of a past when human life was valued. There are now those who wish to erase that memory in order to advance their own social and political objectives.

In the HBO film, actress Sissy Spacek, as Sherri Finkbine, is shown talking to her neighbor. The neighbor says she would have the baby, but Sherri says, "You're being a saint, thinking about everyone but yourself."

We could use more saints and fewer selfish people. The handicapped (or "physically challenged," in the lexicon of political correctness) are not a burden. They are a blessing to many whose lives have been enriched by them. Their lives matter to them and to those who love them. Ask them. They'll tell you. HBO wouldn't ask and wasn't interested because the response might have subverted the purpose of the film. In not asking, HBO has helped make selfishness appear more attractive than sainthood.

LIVING (AND DYING) IN AMERICA

Among the questions First Lady Hillary Rodham Clinton wants answered in the debate she began by heading up a health care task force is, What are the parameters for the beginning and ending of life?

This is a totally modern question, one asked primarily by the children of the sixties. It is based on a flawed philosophy which demands that medicine and science serve the ends of that philosophy, not the reverse. So, even though sophisticated cameras can peek inside the womb, even photographing, as *Life* magazine has done, the actual moment of conception, the little "gods" and "goddesses" conceived in the philosophy of the sixties ask us to ignore what we can see with our own eyes and believe what they tell us.

In the matter of *Roe* v. *Wade* (perhaps the most divisive and contentious Supreme Court decision since Dred Scott a century ago, in which blacks were denied full classification as human beings worthy of constitutional protection), the right to life of the unborn was declared null and void and a new standard was arbitrarily determined. That standard was "viability," which differs from child to child and which is effectively not a sufficient excuse to ban abortion because the courts have ruled that the "health," even the "mental health," of the mother is sufficient reason to obtain an abortion, no matter the status of the pregnancy. Of course, the abortion "doctor" is not about to lose a customer, so it is rare that he or she turns one away.

Abortion was supposed to free women from the "burdens" of their gender. Women get pregnant. Men don't. So, in order for women to feel as fully free as men, women must be allowed to become "unpregnant" if they wish, for whatever reason.

In arguing from such a base, women are reclassifying themselves into something less than men, something less than human, because they are sacrificing their unique biological and psychological roles as mothers on the altar of convenience, based on a lie that they will be better off without the "burden" of an "unwanted" child.

While there are some women who continue to use such terms, even several years after their abortions, many have suppressed guilt feelings that have yet to come out. Of those whose feelings have finally emerged and with whom I have talked, there have been suicide attempts, deep depression, and profound guilt once they have come to grips with what they have done.

Because television refuses to interview these women, it dupes other women into believing the lie that abortion is the answer to a serious problem, not the compounding many times over of a problem for which help is now readily available at crisis pregnancy centers scattered throughout the country.

The abortion wars are now more than twenty years old, with no end in sight. The reason is that abortion, like many other social ills, is the result of individual moral choices. Abortion hasn't corrupted us; we have abortion because we have allowed ourselves to become corrupted. It is the ultimate act of selfishness, which says, "I want to have sex whenever I wish, outside or inside of marriage, and if I happen to get pregnant and don't want to be, I will play God and kill my child."

Pro-lifers can continue to chant the same mantras on mostly deaf ears, or they can adopt a new strategy in fighting a practice that most Americans think should not be performed.

A University of Texas professor of journalism, Marvin Olasky, has offered a wise suggestion. He wants to apply diplomat George Kennan's anti-Communist policy of containment to the abortion war. In a *Foreign Affairs* article he wrote in 1947, Kennan said that instead of engaging in military adventures against communism, the United States should concentrate on the "long-term, patient but firm and vigilant containment of Russian expansive tendencies."

Olasky's point is that great evil, be it communism or the destruction of innocent human life, if contained and not allowed to spread, will ultimately self-destruct. "The pro-life goal," he writes, "should be to help Americans see abortion not as a right but a rite, a nonnormative practice engaged in by sidestream groups and not given societal approval. As abortion is contained in that way, the provision of compassionate alternatives will reduce the likelihood of abortion being used as a desperate recourse."

Focusing on laws alone will not produce the results pro-lifers seek or have much effect on a country that continues to drench itself in sensuality and immorality (reflected hourly on television, in what has become the funeral dirge of the culture—popular music—and in motion pictures that equate premarital and extramarital intercourse with romance, excitement, and fulfillment).

Containment and eventual rollback will be far more effective, but it will require a unity heretofore unseen among pro-lifers, many of whom hurt their own cause with an absolutism that may make them feel self-assured, but does nothing to reduce the number of abortions.

If pro-lifers combine a containment policy with a strategy of providing information to women, abortion could go the way of slavery. As with slavery, though, its elimination just might take a century or more to accomplish.

PART SIX

"STAR-SPANGLED BANNER"

Jimi Hendrix, Woodstock

CHAPTER 8

The Promise
of Progressive
Education

A government survey that took five years and was published in late 1993 found that 90 million Americans—nearly half the adult population—read and write so poorly that it is difficult for them to hold a decent job. Their deficiencies make it hard to perform such tasks as calculating the difference in price of two items and filling out a Social Security form.

Many of these adults, said the survey, cannot write a brief letter explaining an error on a credit card bill. Neither can they figure out a Saturday departure on a bus schedule or use a calculator to determine the difference between a sale price and a regular price.

The question that must be asked after reading this report is how an education system into which billions of tax dollars have been poured, and continue to be poured, could do such a terrible job of equipping modern Americans with the basic skills they need to think and work adequately and effectively. The education establishment has committed fraud on the American people, taking our tax dollars and promising a return for them, but failing to deliver the goods.

What has happened to America's once-great education system? As recently as thirty years ago, enabling students to make a living and make a life were seen as related and essential objectives of the education system. While these remain the stated objectives, the ingredients necessary to produce the finished product have been replaced by other, more politically and socially "correct" ingredients that contribute, along with other factors, to the "dumbing down" of many children who have been robbed of their education birthright.

Such views are no longer heard only in "right-wing" circles. Growing numbers of parents, frustrated by the inability or unwillingness of too many schools to teach essentials, also feel this way.

Even respected educators are beginning to speak up.

Dr. Ernest Boyer, president of the Carnegie Foundation for the Advancement of Teaching, and Dr. Theodore Sizer, director of the Coalition for Essential Schools, are taking what once would have been considered an extremist view. They predict that public and business leaders are so frustrated by the poor condition of contemporary American education that they will abandon public schools in the next decade.

This, they say, will leave a system of private schools, elite suburban public schools, and a few dismal urban public schools filled with the neediest students.

The views of Boyer and Sizer were detailed in a front-page story in the May 11, 1993, edition of the *Dallas Morning News*.

"I don't think educators know how angry people are," said Sizer. "Their patience has just about run out."

Secretary of Education Richard Riley was more blunt. In a telephone interview with the paper, Riley said that the schools are on a path to mediocrity "that would be absolutely damaging for this great country."

Sizer and Boyer agreed that parents and other segments of the public must reach a consensus on reforms to make schools work. But they were pessimistic that such a consensus could be reached before the public system fails.

In Minneapolis, things have gotten so bad and public officials have grown so frustrated over the way their schools are operating that the Minneapolis School Board voted in November 1993 to turn over management of all city schools to a private consulting firm. It is believed to be the first such arrangement in the country.

The chief executive officer of Public Strategies Group, Inc., the organization that will take over operations, is Babak Armalani. He said, "There is a growing feeling here in Minneapolis and all over the country that the current bureaucratic system of running a school is antiquated."

Under the proposal, Public Strategies will receive a flat fee and earn a profit if it operates the system less expensively. While this plan deals mostly with the operation of the school system, if it works, a change in what is taught and how it is taught is likely to come next.

Once there was general agreement on what students should be taught and what truth was and how it could be discovered. But education became another tool of sixties activists to indoctrinate this and future generations in their failed philosophy, lifestyles, and worldview. Schools were rapidly transformed into laboratories in which young human guinea pigs were inoculated with a philosophy alien to this country.

All debates should begin with definitions of terms. Reading the definition of "educate" reveals how far we have drifted from the standard: "To develop mentally, morally, or aesthetically . . . to persuade or condition to feel, believe, or act in a desired way or to accept something as desirable."

Within the memory of many now alive, to develop mentally meant to pursue not just facts, but wisdom. To develop morally was to accept certain standards proven to work, such as the principles contained in the Ten Commandments and the Sermon on the Mount and such concepts as honesty, fidelity, self-control, personal responsibility for one's actions, the sacrifice of self-interest in behalf of the interest of others, honor, duty, and love of country.

Now, what passes for education consists of assimilating

"information," not truths, taught by an army of propagandists who begin with certain assumptions about history (it was dominated by dead white males and so we must rewrite and reinterpret it through the prism of the contemporary political framework called "political correctness"); about science (the only truth we can discover is that taught to us by science, and Carl Sagan is right—the cosmos is all there is, was, or will be); about life ("your parents are dumb; listen to your teachers and counselors instead; we know what is best for you; here, have a condom").

It is not just the average student who continues to be "dumbed down" by government schools. Gifted children are also getting short shrift.

In a study on gifted children by the Department of Education, it was revealed that hundreds of thousands of bright American students are sitting bored in classes in which teachers rehash lessons the students have already learned.

Feeding the lack of challenge to the estimated two million brightest students is what the study refers to as "America's ambivalence toward the intellect" that makes some pupils not want to excel for fear of being branded a "dweeb."

But it goes deeper than that. It turns out there is a "politically correct" reason for not encouraging gifted students. According to a story in the November 5, 1993, *Washington Post*, "Since the 1970s, federal officials have shied from the topic of gifted students because of controversy over the definition of 'gifted' and concern that so few minorities were included in accelerated programs. Private foundations and public school budgets hesitated to fund enrichment programs for the brightest because it was seen as 'politically incorrect' to seek money and attention for the best students when so many students were failing."

Harvard education professor Howard Gardner is one who decries the present state of affairs, calling it "malpractice for kids who are brilliant in mathematics to have to sit around and diddle."

This is a classic example of the socialistic mind-set that grips most liberals. Just as liberals adopt a take-from-the-rich-to-subsidize-the-poor policy, in education they seek to make everyone equally mediocre because they fear success, achievement, and greatness. Why? Because of a mentality that causes them to see people in terms of categories and classes and not as individuals with unique characteristics who should be given not equality of outcome, but equality of opportunity.

It now appears education may be moving from the grotesque to the absurd. The *Washington Times* reported in its June 22, 1993, edition on a meeting of the National Women's Studies Association at the University of Maryland in College Park. The university is home to one of four hundred "curriculum transformation projects" on campuses across America that are designed to change student thinking on a number of subjects.

Deborah Rosenfelt, a professor of women's studies at the University of Maryland, says the agenda is a natural outgrowth of what is happening in public schools: "Multiculturalism in public schools is focused on race and ethnicity," she says. "At the university level, it began in women's studies, with some intersections of race and ethnicity."

And what can students and their parents, who usually subsidize their children's college educations, look forward to getting for their time and money at more and more of our colleges and universities? At the University of Maryland conference, attended by seven hundred administrators, teachers, and students, there was heavy emphasis on one subject: lesbianism.

Presentations included "Teaching Queer: Incorporating Gay and Lesbian Perspectives into Introductory Courses"; "Lesbian Feminism in the Academy"; "Lesbian Perspectives on/in Literature"; "Lesbian Theory in Poetry"; "Initial Reactions to Lesbian Feminist Literary Criticism"; a film called "L Is for the Way You Look," described as a "playful exploration of lesbian history and the women who have served as role models and objects of desire for young lesbians"; "Dykeotomy," a video that examines how "lesbians and gay men form an identity when language and rituals assume heterosexuality"; and "Juggling Gender," described as a "loving portrait of Jennifer Miller, a lesbian performer who lives her life with a full beard."

During the Fall 1993/Spring 1994 term at the small Washington College in Chestertown, Maryland, you could take a course for credit called "Pornography in the U.S." Professor R. C. De Prospo offered the nightly two-and-a-half-hour class to consider pornographic films and literature, including Sharon Stone's performance as Catherine in *Basic Instinct*, a film that makes a big deal of Stone's character's not wearing panties.

For an idea of what might be taught in such a course and in similar courses at universities throughout the country, one might have looked in on a gathering of 11,000 professors of language and literature held in New York City from December 27 to 30, 1992. They attended the 108th convention of the Modern Language Association.

According to the convention's official program, among the lectures presented were some that sought to undermine the principles of American culture in favor of "multiculturalism," which suggests that no culture is superior to any other. So, professors were offered "Multiculturalism: The Task of Literary Representation in the Twenty-first Century." Other lectures were about sex, demons and witches, and submission and perversion. One paper presented was titled, "Performing Lesbian Sadomasochism."

Race, sex, and gender seemed to dominate, and if you were a straight, white, heterosexual male, this gathering was designed to make you feel out of place, guilty, and oppressive.

On December 28, a morning session titled "Can Popular Culture Be Politically Correct" included a leadoff paper called "Don't Worry about Being Right." That seemed tame compared to what followed, which included "Transvestite Biography," "Cruisin' for a Bruisin'," and "The Ins and Outs of Lesbian Sex." The latter was part of a session titled "Lesbian Tongues Untied."

As one reads the rest of the program, these sessions were not exceptions, but seemed to dominate the convention.

There was "Vegetarianism and Social Reform," "Beheading Scenes and Gender Assertion," "Homophile and Necrophile," "Rewriting Genesis, Rewriting Sophocles," "Reading the Lesbian in Black and Jewish Women's Literature," and, for the history majors, "Effeminization and Miscegenation in Tudor England."

There were scores more. There were even separate cash bars for radicals, women, Indians, and gays and lesbians. How could one keep up?

The program goes on and on: "Feminist Jurisprudence," "Lesbians at the Opera," "Incest Is Best," "With Your Tongue Down My Throat," "Dead Male Bodies," "My Vampire, My Friend."

Was this a convention just to allow professors to let off steam, or will what was taught here filter its way down (if one can go further down than this) to influence the minds and spirits of adolescents in the classrooms of these professors?

Why do I think lectures and courses like these, or a degree in women's studies with a major in lesbianism, just might not prepare someone to compete with, say, the Japanese in the next century?

As for learning about a moral code in school, one by which people should live in order to benefit themselves and society, the notion that such a moral code even exists, or ought to exist, has been abandoned.

No wonder frustrated parents turned intellectual Allan Bloom's 1987 book about failing public education into a best-seller. In *The Closing of the American Mind: How Higher Education Has Failed Democracy and Impoverished the Souls of*

Today's Students, Bloom exposed the fault line running to some degree through all modern public education: "There is one thing a professor can be absolutely certain of: Almost every student entering the university believes, or says he believes, that truth is relative. . . . The danger they have been taught to fear from absolutism is not error, but intolerance. Relativism is necessary to openness, and this is the virtue, the only virtue, which all primary education for more than fifty years has dedicated itself to inculcating.

"Openness—and the relativism that makes it the only plausible stance in the face of various claims to truth and various ways of life and kinds of human beings—is the great insight of our times. The true believer is the real danger. The study of history and of culture teaches that all the world was mad in the past; men always thought they were right, and that led to wars, persecutions, slavery, xenophobia, racism, and chauvinism. The point is not to correct the mistakes and really be right; rather it is not to think you are right at all."

Discipline, of course, died at home before it was buried at school. The discipline breakdown followed the breakup of too many marriages and the proliferation of too many child-indulgent parents. Even so, we have redefined childrearing. We now expect children to catch our values the way they catch a cold.

Children do not "catch" values any more than they "assimilate" vaccines, which must be injected into their bloodstream or taken by mouth in order to ward off disease. Values, personal and national, must be drummed into children so they will think and act in ways that promote American interests, and their own.

FROM "GOOD MORNING, TEACHER" TO "SHUT UP, BITCH"

The restructuring of modern public education, which acquired most of its momentum in the sixties, has been in place long enough to give it a grade.

It gets an F.

Not only has public education failed miserably to fulfill its grandiose promises, it now appears to focus more on advancing social agendas than on teaching standards—both of knowledge and of conduct.

A fourteen-year-old freshman at McLean High School in northern Virginia told the *Washington Post* about an encounter he had with one of his teachers: "I lost my temper and cursed the teacher. I was talking to one of my friends, and [the teacher] said something like 'Shut up' and it pissed me off and I said, 'Go to hell. [Expletive] you.'"

Seventeen-year-old Gisela Aponte, a junior at McLean, said she tried to explain to her teacher why she was late for class "and she started going off on me about what I needed to do to get to class on time. I just freaked out and called her the 'B' word. I said, 'Shut up, bitch.' I got Saturday detention, but I don't regret it. She deserved to be called that."

Pat McIntosh, a counselor at Glasgow Middle School in Fairfax County, Virginia, explained to the *Post* why he thinks many students talk this way to teachers: "They get upset when they are told not to do something. They will say '[Expletive] you' in a minute, or 'Get out of my face. You touch me again and I'm going to knock you out.'"

Connie Shephard teaches American history and government in Orange County, California. After several years' absence from teaching, she returned to the classroom to be confronted by a sixteen-year-old who told her in class, "Shut the f—— up, you bitch."

In a column she wrote for the April 18, 1993, op-ed page

of the *Los Angeles Times*, Shephard raised some important questions: "Where was I when the classroom made the giant leap from 'Good Morning, Miss Landers,' to 'Don't mess with me, bitch'? [I've learned] that homework is obsolete, tardiness is the rule, not the exception, and if I have any desire at all of surviving until lunch, discipline is my first priority."

Connie Shephard thinks, correctly, that what we have here is a failure to communicate with our children: "As we calmly sit by 'listening' to our children, trying to 'relate' to their problems, allowing them 'space' to find themselves, attempting to 'reason' with their every argument, we are not teaching them that sometimes life is hard, that it's all right and even normal to be depressed from time to time, and that there is something intrinsically rewarding in hard work and sacrifice.

"Instead, we scratch our heads in disbelief at a generation given everything, but which understands nothing. A generation that we expect to run the future government but which can't get to class on time. A generation we expect to manage future industry but which can't read, let alone fill out a job application. A generation we expect to carry on our American tradition but which has no idea what that tradition is, and if asked to defend it would find it just too much work."

THE UNENLIGHTENED ENLIGHTENMENT

There are essentially two views of Man (or human beings, if you prefer the gender-neutral or inclusive language). One is that we evolved from primordial ooze into fish and then monkeys and are now what we are. As part of the animal kingdom, we can be trained, like animals, to act and think in ways that would be considered good by the majority, though we have no objective standard by which to measure "good" other than a contemporary prevailing majority opinion.

The second view derives from the Judeo-Christian philosophy that Man was created in the image of God, but fell and is now damaged by what is known as a "sin nature." Having such a nature means that Man is not basically good and so must either be constrained by an inner sense of an almighty God to whom one is accountable in this life and the next and from whom one may receive a new nature in a direct encounter with Jesus Christ, or controlled from without by the state, acting as God's surrogate, conforming people to a minimal standard of "righteousness" in order that the general welfare might be promoted.

Modern public education, until early in this century, used to be based primarily on the second view, and lessons in history, biology, and even English ("A" is for Adam, "B" is for Beelzebub) reflected that worldview. In fact, a knowledge of God, familiarity with the Ten Commandments, and development of a religious life and the personal and social sensibilities that went with such a life were considered an integral part of a true American education.

Somewhere around the late 1940s, after World War II, things began to subtly change. As the great migration to the suburbs and away from old neighborhoods and tight-knit families began, there was a sense that education should be more "progressive" or "modern." Some educators, who had long shared the views of John Dewey and other "progressives," leapt at the opportunity to transform education the way television and refrigerator manufacturers were modernizing the American home.

They began to promote a philosophy of education based on a principle of human nature promulgated during the Enlightenment.

The Enlightenment was anything but enlightening. It was a reaction by European intellectuals to the Reformation period that preceded it. Unlike those of the Reformation, Enlightenment thinkers believed that people and society were perfectable. They rejected the existence of, or accountability to, a Creator-God. The lack of any absolute by which to judge men's actions led to the bloodbath of the French Revolution and later the Bolshevik Revolution in Russia.

As an autonomous creature, Man was then free to establish his own laws and morals and to change them at any time to suit the prevailing philosophical winds of his age.

As Francis Schaeffer defined it in *How Should We Then Live?*, the Enlightenment was a utopian dream that was thoroughly secular in its thinking. "The humanistic elements which had risen during the Renaissance [which directly preceded the Reformation] came to flood tide in the Enlightenment," wrote Schaeffer. "Here was man starting from himself absolutely. And if the humanistic elements of the Renaissance stand in sharp contrast to the Reformation, the Enlightenment was in total antithesis to it. The two stood for and were based upon absolutely different things in an absolute way, and they produced absolutely different results."

And what is this "humanism" that so pervades contemporary public education? It is the Enlightenment's chief bequest to modern man, as Schaeffer defined it: "Man beginning from himself, with no knowledge except what he himself can discover and no standards outside of himself. In this view Man is the measure of all things as the Enlightenment expressed it."

Frederick Moore Vinson, Earl Warren's predecessor as Chief Justice, was an ideological descendant of the Enlightenment and demonstrated the curse of this philosophy insofar as the law is concerned when he said, "Nothing is more certain in modern society than the principle that there are no absolutes." A statement, I presume, he meant absolutely.

It wasn't that all who believed (or believe) in Enlightenment principles are atheists who couldn't (or can't) wait to get their hands on the minds and spirits of young children to damn them to intellectual and spiritual perdition. The point is that there are principles associated with these antithetical views of Man, principles that are themselves antithetical to one another. They lead in different directions because they proceed from different origins.

If our closest relative is downtown at the zoo, then certain views about Man and God flow from that belief. Conversely, if there is a personal God who is knowable and who has set down certain rules for the benefit of those He has created, there are ideas that flow from this belief as well. It is incorrect to say that the Enlightenment view of Man is more tolerant, pluralistic, and open-minded than the other view. If that were so, why do those whose views have been fashioned by the Enlightenment philosophy try so diligently to exclude any and all references to the other worldview? The "absolute truth" is this: By acknowledging the objective existence of God and sin, one recognizes something that is essential to the achievement of true self-esteem. That is because without a higher state—or better condition—to aspire to beyond this poor, wretched, rotting one that leads to death, all notions of worth become temporary, relative, and ultimately meaningless. Most people (whether or not they accept spiritual definitions and theological truths) would prefer to think of themselves as existing for reasons other than taking up space on the planet and contributing to the landfill. But culture increasingly wars against the transcendent and pretends that when it is victorious, humankind will applaud and rejoice over its victory. In fact, such victory only leads to despair.

The failure to teach the presence of absolutes and truth in our schools is what is primarily responsible for the education disaster that nearly everyone now sees or forecasts for the near future. If all values are primarily derived from the mind of Man and can change with the times or the next opinion poll, then why should students accept any value the state tries to teach them, since it may be as outmoded as their computer in the near future? For that matter, why even get out of bed in the morning, if there is no purpose for living beyond acquiring things? "He Who Dies with the Most Toys Wins," proclaims the bumper sticker. But wins what?

If a philosophy and worldview once produced generations of young people who could read, write, and think while resisting, for the most part, the temptation to engage in anti-social and personally corrupting behavior, why doesn't it make sense to return to that philosophy and reject the one that has brought us crack cocaine in the school yard and drive-by shootings at the playground?

I HAVE SEEN THE EDUCATIONAL
FUTURE AND IT STINKS

If you don't like what the recent past has given us in the name of education, you're going to positively hate the future.

They're building it in Iowa, and think that if they build it there, people will come to accept it everywhere.

It's called "multicultural, nonsexist education," or MCNSE. Since 1988, the Iowa legislature has passed a series of laws that mandate the teaching of MCNSE, not only in Iowa's public schools, but in accredited private and even religious schools. Schools must teach MCNSE unless they decline accreditation.

The question to ask when considering this and similar curricula founded on radical left-wing politics, not real education, is whether it will equip young people for real jobs. Do the Japanese or Germans take this approach to education? They most certainly do not.

MCNSE requires that the approach to all education should be "global." This means that children must not think more highly of their state or nation than of any other state or nation. All states and nations are equal. National pride, even regional pride, is counterproductive and injurious. Instead, students will "acquire a *realistic* perspective on world issues and problems, and prospects for an awareness of the relationship between an individual's self-interest and the concerns of people everywhere in the world." (emphasis mine)

Will cheering for your favorite college or high school team soon be considered too prideful an exercise for students to engage in?

"At-risk" students whose "aspirations and achievement may be negatively affected by stereotypes linked to race, national origin, language background, gender, income, family status, and disability" will be identified and given special consideration.

I'll bet. "I'm from the government and I'm here to help you" never looked like such an empty promise.

MCNSE is not unique to Iowa. Activists are pursuing similar agendas by other names in other states. It is a formula for dismantling the uniqueness and strength of America. The individual parts will become more important than the whole and young people will be taught that their value is not defined by their own worth, but by the language, gender, or ethnic group to which they belong.

Imagine what such a view would have produced in our seven-decade war against the enemies of this century: communism, fascism, and the imperial empire that was Japan.

A culture is defined by its collective ideals and ideas, its values and beliefs, which distinguish it from other cultures that may share different, even opposite values and beliefs. In the past, immigrants were attracted to America and blended into our culture. They wanted to become, and largely succeeded in becoming, Americans. Now the danger is we will become balkanized or hyphenated Americans and lose our uniqeness and national identity. Our national motto is in danger of being changed from "out of many, one" (*e pluribus unum*) to "out of one, many."

Academic freedom will be sacrificed and MCNSE will be imposed by the state for what is regarded as our collective good. Included in the Iowa MCNSE program is mandatory sex education. This is the response by the members of the sixties generation to their own failed morality. Rather than restore the standard of right and wrong, they assert that education about how to have "safe sex" will do the trick. It is like providing getaway cars for bank robbers rather than teaching why it is wrong to stick up a bank.

The MCNSE program includes an "optional" manual for the sex education curriculum that recommends using "anatomically correct" words. Teachers are told to become comfortable with these words so that they might use them without embarrassment in class. "The words penis, vagina, breasts, etc. should be as common to the teacher of human sexuality as senate, legislator, representative, etc. are to the teacher of government." This is from the *Human Growth and Development* manual. The sex education curriculum is designed to begin in kindergarten and continue through twelfth grade.

Multiculturalism is really not about education at all. It dumbs down, dilutes, and makes illegitimate that which has made American culture unique. As American values have triumphed around the world, multiculturalists want to abandon that which the rest of the world is rushing to embrace.

Pluralism of values quickly leads to a valueless society. It says there is no truth, no clear objective or moral order worth pursuing. It allows others to create the agenda for America and, in fact, to form an imperfect union, which leads to disunity. Multiculturalists want to divide this house, which then will not be able to stand.

Such a radical political agenda could never be implemented without the de facto submission of people who do not share the official position of the state of Iowa and the multiculturalists. If parents who have a different worldview, morals, and values would pull their children out of public schools and educate them either at home or in private or religious schools, the grip of the multiculturalists on education would be broken.

To paraphrase another Iowan, Meredith Willson, the late composer of *The Music Man*: Friends, either you're closing your eyes to a situation you do not wish to acknowledge, or you are not aware of the caliber of disaster indicated by the presence of multiculturalism in your community.

Sure, students should learn about other nations, races, creeds, and histories, but not at the expense of those things we once held dear. MCNSE will shape America into a type of intellectual, social, and moral Third World nation, and the people running MCNSE will become the equivalent of tinhorn dictators.

TRICKLEDOWN MATRICULATION

By the time the graduate of a modern public school gets to the university, he or she is supposed to be ready for the practical application of all that has been "learned" in those hothouses of liberalism. Modern university professors will now make sure that these little acorns grow into giant liberal, humanistic oaks.

I don't receive many invitations to speak at universities anymore, because I do not affirm the accepted orthodoxies of supposedly "higher" education. Those who claim to be the protectors of "academic freedom" and "pluralism" fear that one voice of reason might undo all they have done to indoctrinate their students.

But someone slipped up and invited me to Bowdoin College in Brunswick, Maine, in early December 1990, where I spoke on "Liberalism and the University."

Bowdoin College is like many other colleges and universities where there are efforts afoot to outlaw certain forms of speech that offend the prevailing orthodoxy and the high priests of academia. Any accusation—no matter how spurious—of sexism, racism, homophobia, ethnocentrism, even speciesism, can be grounds for harassment, mistreatment, and possible expulsion.

I told the students at Bowdoin that after speaking on more than eighty college campuses during the last ten years, I had concluded that on most of those campuses the harmless absurdities of the past (like packing a phone booth) had given way to modern outrages, such as political indoctrination, that are becoming the norm.

I cited some examples. A week-long program of workshops and panels was held at Harvard under the title AWARE (Actively Working Against Racism and Ethnocentrism). It included a former Dartmouth dean who suggested that Dartmouth and Harvard were "genocidal in nature" because of their attitudes toward racial issues. A Harvard professor at the conference said that one should never "introduce any sort of thing that might hurt a group" into a classroom because "the pain that insensitivity can create is more important than a professor's academic freedom."

Some of the new-wave restrictions on "backward" attitudes are silly and sanctimonious. The Harvard Office of Race Relations and Minority Affairs, which originated the AWARE conference, called for a ban on fifties nostalgia parties—the kind with poodle skirts and "Rock Around the Clock" music—because racism had been rampant in that decade.

Many universities that once taught critical thinking based on a set of core principles now teach things that are unrelated to reality. Some professors believe that tenure has placed them above accountability. Any attempt to critique their teaching is viewed as tampering with holy writ and a blasphemy against academia.

Many universities have lost not only the ability, but the will to guide students, because they don't know where these students are headed and are afraid to find out. They offer cafeteria-style education, in which students are free to consume a variety of intellectual junk food and to attempt to find meaning and direction in life without definitions or a map.

Parents should be more discerning about where they will subsidize their children's education. They care about the quality of food the school serves their offspring. They should care at least as much, maybe more, about what is going into their minds.

That's what I told the students who came to hear me lecture at Bowdoin College. Not all were persuaded, but they listened, a courtesy I was not paid during a 1981 appearance at Smith College, a bastion of supposed "tolerance," where they booed and cursed me from start to finish and a group of lesbians sat in the front row, holding hands and kissing each other throughout my talk.

WE DON'T NEED NO EDUCATION

One of the rock group Pink Floyd's many contributions to the lowering of American culture to sewer level was a "song" called "Another Brick in the Wall." One of the song's lines was, "We don't need no education." It should be the national anthem of modern American public education, and a reminder of what that education has produced.

What America desperately needs is freedom of choice on education. If we can have freedom of choice on abortion, why not freedom of choice on education for those fortunate enough to have been born?

The answer is that powerful unions and the education lobby are interested in controlling the minds, hearts, and bodies of children. It is the only way they can be sure of rearing substantial numbers of liberals to replace themselves.

Liberalism must be indoctrinated. It is not naturally acquired through observation and experience. Liberalism exists only in the minds of goofy professors and other elitists who think they are smarter and better than everyone else. When liberalism is applied, it never produces its advertised claims. An often-heard joke is that communism is dying worldwide and the only place you can still find high concentrations of Communists (outside of China) is in American universities.

School choice would change all that and make public education, if it survives into the twenty-first century, accountable to parents whose children are not its hostages.

Numerous polls over several years have revealed that Americans favor school choice, including private and religious schools, by wide margins.

In the fall of 1991, an Arnold Steinberg poll for *Reason Magazine* asked eight hundred registered California voters whether state money should follow a child to the public or private, religious or secular school of his parents' choice. Respondents favored school choice by about 2:1.

In the November 2, 1993, elections, school choice was defeated in California largely because of a multimillion-dollar disinformation campaign conducted on television by the National Education Association and the California Teachers Association. But school choice is going national as many other states consider the issue, and a new group, Americans for School Choice, whose founders include former education secretaries Lamar Alexander and William Bennett, plans to keep the subject before the public.

Reasons for parental support of school choice are typical of what other polls and surveys have discovered in other states. Seventy percent of the Californians surveyed were disappointed with the performance of public schools. They also were surprised to learn the average annual cost of $5,242 to educate a California public school student.

Respondents believed allowing parents to choose which schools their children would attend would make schools more accountable to parents, limit increases in spending because schools would become more efficient, better assist low-income and minority students, and motivate teachers, offering them greater freedom to teach effectively.

When parents talk about favoring education choice, two reasons always loom large. One is that most people believe an education is not complete unless it instills a moral code and a value system in a child. A majority believe this is best accomplished in a private or religious school.

A second reason is that parents notice that although more money is being spent on education, it is producing less satisfactory results.

In the early nineties, Scholastic Aptitude Test (SAT) verbal scores were at their lowest level nationally in history. Yet spending on education, according to federal figures, reached a record $413.8 billion in the fall of 1991. About $248.6 billion of that total went to public primary and secondary education, making the average per-pupil investment just under $6,000 annually.

One of the Education Department's "Back to School" forecasts, which it issues at the start of every school year, showed that per-pupil spending in the public schools increased nearly $3,000 between the early eighties and the early nineties. For this increased spending, the national verbal SAT score fell in the early nineties to an all-time low of 422. That was 44 points below its 1967 high of 466. In math, the SAT score in the early nineties was 474. In 1967, the math score was 492, an 18-point difference.

In state after state, increased spending on education has generally paralleled declining achievement.

Yet, during that same period, private religious schools recorded a combined math and verbal score of 909. That is 13 points above the national average. Independent private schools registered a combined score of 994, or 98 points above the national average.

There is no connection, despite politicians' and the education lobby's constant assertions, between the amount of money spent by states and improved test scores. Utah spent $2,629 per student in 1991, but achieved one of the highest combined SAT scores in the nation: 1,031. Washington, D.C., spent $7,550 per student and achieved the second-lowest score: 880.

Choice is the answer. Arguments about church-state separation are bogus. If the government accepts money from religious and nonreligious citizens, if it subsidizes "art" through the National Endowment for the Arts, which many religious people believe is anti-God, then why shouldn't that money be allowed to follow a child to the school of his and his parents' choosing, particularly if that school produces an intellectually superior, psychologically sound, and ethically principled person?

The education establishment has another agenda. So does Congress, much of which is beholden to the education lobby, which contributes money to the campaigns of friendly members. It will be up to the public, then, to demand freedom of choice for education. Those who can afford it are already getting out. The moderate-to-poor-income people deserve a chance to abandon the sinking ship as well.

THE COMING INTELLECTUAL
AND MORAL REBELLION

Only two roads remain for America. One, which we have been traveling down for three decades, leads to destruction because it entails intellectual, moral, and cultural collapse.

The other road leads to rebellion against the status quo and a refusal to accept it as the way things are or ought to be.

Some are predicting the rebellion is closer than anyone thinks.

William Kristol, former chief of staff to Dan Quayle, who now directs the "Bradley Project on the Nineties," and his associate, Jay Lefkowitz, believe a new revolt is brewing in the country, even as liberals begin to feel smug about their people returning to power in the White House.

Kristol and Lefkowitz predict a revolt by parents that will "shake the halls of power as forcefully as did the tax revolt that began in the early seventies."

Writing in *New Perspectives Quarterly*, they say, ". . . the story of the last half of the seventies was not one of liberalism triumphant. The real story turned out to be the rise of a tax-payers' revolt against liberal government, a rebellion that featured antitax initiatives in several states and fueled the election of Ronald Reagan in 1980."

Where the taxpayer revolt stood in 1974, the two write, the parents' revolt stands now. "On the surface, a liberal president and Congress dominate the scene, infatuated with grand visions of a new era of activist government. And the doctrines of liberalism seem more politically correct than ever before.

"But if we look deeper, we see a different picture. Across the nation, parents of all races and classes are rebelling on behalf of their children against the education and social service bureaucracies that, parents believe, squander their money and scorn their values. This parents' revolt has, until now, mostly simmered beneath the surface. But there have been occasional eruptions."

Kristol and Lefkowitz cite several examples. One was a nationally covered rebellion by parents in Queens, New York, against an edict by the school chancellor to impose a "rainbow curriculum" on first-graders that included gay rights subjects. The parents succeeded in getting the chancellor voted out of office. In Milwaukee, citizens overwhelmingly defeated a referendum supported by the city's leaders to build more public schools, and an advocate for parental rights came close to winning an upset victory in Wisconsin's school superintendent race. In Chicago, inner-city parents lobbied the state legislature and filed suit in court to claim their right to choose a decent education for their children.

The key to a successful rebellion is the realization by parents that they do not have to accept the status quo or be bullied by elites who think they know better than parents how and what children should be taught. Like taxpayers who banded together and were of one mind to successfully lead the tax revolt of the seventies, so now can parents do the same with education.

Kristol and Lefkowitz say the parent revolt must move beyond anger and outrage "toward a more coherent agenda," which must include parental choice on where their children are to be educated and parental input as to what is taught.

If school choice succeeds nationally, the power of the education elites is doomed, and the prospects for real education are greatly enhanced. And "it is the public school establishment," write Kristol and Lefkowitz, "that undergirds the edifice of social service providers who seem to be usurping the proper role of parents."

All this movement needs is a national spokesperson who will lead it. The troops are there. The issues are in focus. If a national leader emerges who can articulate the aspirations of parents for their children, he (or she) could ride this horse all the way to the White House and bring changes in Congress that could last for generations to come.

CHAPTER 9

The Promise That Bigger Government Will Do It All for You

Big Government is like Pac-Man, gobbling up everything in its path. It resembles an old Japanese movie monster, consuming America and its resources.

The Virginia county in which I live, not content with taxing my property, my house, and my home office (including desk, lamp, and computer), is now taxing my brain. It forced me to get a business license. I pointed out that I don't sell cars or frozen yogurt. Doesn't matter, I was told. Even though my ideas aren't tangible, the county thinks they should be taxed. I called my lawyer. He said I could fight it in federal court with no guarantees I would win. The cost for a federal lawsuit? Between $10,000 and $20,000. I paid $500 for the business license.

This is Big Government run amok.

Big and ever-growing government is the most visible example of an incorrect view of the human condition. When such notions as sin, redemption, and compassion (as a human trait, not a government component) were discarded by the sixties generation, some force had to be brought in to take care of us, since it was obvious human beings had not yet reached that state of perfection liberals said would be possible if they were given the power to restructure society.

When the Holocaust Museum opened in Washington in the spring of 1993, *Newsweek* magazine, perhaps unwittingly, correctly assessed why government has grown so large.

Writer Kenneth Woodward said in the April 26 issue, "This is a history museum, and the story it tells forever shattered the Enlightenment illusion of human perfectibility."

Later in the same story, writer Cathleen McGuigan reviewed the architecture created by James Ingo Freed. She quoted Freed as saying, "In a way, it's a critique of modernism's lofty ideals, which were supposed to solve man's problems."

Man wrongly diagnosed himself as perfectible, given the right education, a good environment, and proper cultural role models. As these prescriptions increasingly demonstrated failure, government responded by upping the "dosage."

President Bill Clinton has picked up where Lyndon Johnson's "Great Society" left off by proposing perhaps the biggest tax increase in history. Why? Because he believes, like most of the sixties generation, that government is, or ought to be, our keeper.

The Clinton administration's view that government (and not people making responsible decisions for themselves and their families) can correct social flaws was expressed by Housing and Urban Development Secretary Henry Cisneros. In a television interview soon after Clinton took office, Cisneros said, "I think one of the things America has to address very, very squarely is whether or not we can live with continued vast spatial separations between the poorest of our populations, concentrated in public housing in central cities, and the vast difference that exists across our urban geography to the suburbs, which are essentially white.

"What we've got to do is break up the concentrations by making it possible for people to live in newly designed, thoughtfully scaled public housing, negotiated with outlying communities, because many of the problems . . . are a symptom of large concentrations of poor people with few role models and no lift."

Here we go again! This is discredited thinking from the sixties, when it was thought public housing was the answer to the poor's housing problems. It wasn't. Public housing, owned and operated by government, has made problems worse.

In what ought to be another discredited view by now, it is said poverty is caused by environment and therefore if the environment is changed, if people have better "role models," they will change, too. There is nothing here about personal decision-making, about not fathering (and mothering) children while still a teenager, about not using drugs, about taking responsibility for one's own life.

Yes, environment—the family and circumstances into which one is born—can be influential, but it does not have to be decisive. In the past, we focused on success stories, not stories of failure, and we seemed to produce more success. Today, we focus on failure, and that's what we get.

Most people can be persuaded to do what is in their and society's best interests if they are led in the right direction and the culture affirms them in right decision-making, but our culture is doing the reverse in the nineties. When we consider that our role models have changed from people of virtue and integrity to those who reflect the opposite, it is no mystery why poverty persists. Successful athletes and rock stars have replaced successful businesspeople as role models, though the odds of a poor person becoming a rock star or professional athlete is a million to one.

The media play a major role in perpetuating poor role models. I attended Black Expo USA in Washington. Successful black entrepreneurs honored each other for their hard work and risk-taking. These were truly successful people, who were proud of their success. There were no television or newspaper reporters.

The media prefer stories about dead blacks in the streets, not successful blacks on their feet. If the media carry only stories about black criminals and pictures of poor blacks, heads down and in handcuffs, being marched off to the police cruiser, what kind of message does this send to black (and white) America?

Housing Secretary Cisneros's assertion is nothing more than a replay of the sixties and its many failed programs and much-failed philosophy. As Cisneros's predecessor, Jack Kemp, has said, "We fought a war on poverty, and the poor lost." That's because we aimed at the wrong target, which was not externals, but internals, an area government has refused to address.

It is not that government is all bad. The Mississippi River is a beautiful river, but when severe flooding in the summer of 1993 caused it to inundate many towns and farms along its route, it turned ugly. It is the same with government. Limited and inside its "banks," government can be good. But when government floods the country with its schemes and programs and drowns those areas once considered the property of family and faith, then government, too, becomes an enemy.

Government's primary role is to control the lawless and to exercise certain powers granted it by the governed. It is not government's business to redeem or rehabilitate people. That can only be done from within.

People need a reason beyond themselves for living, for working, for contributing to a culture rather than existing only for themselves. When government does things that encourage such notions, it serves noble purposes and increases citizen respect and support. But when government becomes the adversary, even the enemy, of higher ideals and things of the spirit, it becomes a burden to its own people and ceases to fulfill the role the Founders had in mind. The main reason government has frustrated so many is that it has lost the support of those whose worldview gives them a purpose for living beyond this life as well as an objective for living in this life. Though the Founders said nothing about a "separation" between church and state, modern secularists have taken the concept and driven a wedge between God and government.

The Founders believed (and this was the purpose of the First Amendment) that the church needed protection from government, not the reverse.

The fact that we have more people in prison in America than ever before and that the social fault line is wide and expanding does not prove we need more and bigger government. In fact, it is proof that the more and bigger government we have had since the sixties has failed to live up to the promises those who believed in government-as-God made to us.

Modern government believes Man is basically good and that his few faults can be rehabilitated from without. In fact, Man is basically not good (as thousands of years of human history attest) and must be redeemed from within.

The public, which intuitively knows this, is now beginning to awaken to the fraudulent concept of government-as-redeemer. But the Clinton administration continues to keep the outmoded faith. Joe Klein writes in *Newsweek* (also April 26, 1993), "Clinton seems to favor worthy but marginally successful antipoverty programs like Head Start and summer jobs (funneled through corroded urban bureaucracies) over crime prevention. This is anachronistic, standard-issue liberalism, and the clearest indication yet that his social priorities are at variance with the public's."

It is one of the reasons President Clinton's approval ratings took such a steep dive early in his administration. People thought they were getting a different, more centrist president, a "new Democrat." When they saw that Clinton was a tax-and-spend liberal in conservative clothing, they became angry, because they've seen that taxing and spending has not solved our problems and they know that bigger government is not the answer.

PUTTING GOVERNMENT FIRST

Bill Clinton's campaign mantra was "putting people first." He even "wrote" a book using that as the title. But since he's been in office, it is clear that he and Hillary Rodham Clinton, the "vote for him and you get me" copresident, believe in putting government first.

Their theology is that government can and must serve as the redeemer of men, women, and children and that the "rich" (now defined by Clinton as those making more than $200,000 per year) have an obligation to pay more money to government in higher taxes so that government can subsidize the "poor." This is necessary because, by liberal definition, rich people are evil. They are evil because liberals see capital as a fixed amount and if rich people are earning a lot of money, they are "stealing" from the rightful share that belongs to the poor.

This is socialism pure and simple. Never mind that the "rich" work hard for their money. Never mind that most rich people went to school and took risks with their money to build businesses. Somehow, according to the liberal theorists, they became "greedy" and are enjoying their wealth while the "deserving poor" have to do without.

It was not insignificant that in Bill Clinton's Inaugural Address, he called upon us to "sacrifice." Again, this idea is based on the flawed assumption of a fixed amount of money that must be shared equally or people will starve to death. Getting people to accept this bogus philosophy is essential if even more taxpayers are to be persuaded to allow government to regularly pick our pockets.

One of the major reasons why it is so difficult to reduce government spending is the size of both government itself and the industries and lobbying organizations that suck from its numerous teats.

According to the Bureau of Labor Statistics, more than

18,578,000 people were working for government at all levels at the beginning of 1993. Nearly three million of those worked for the federal government. This compares to 108,434,000 in private, nonagricultural jobs.

It may be the first time in history—it is certainly the first time since 1946—that there have been more people on government payrolls than in manufacturing. In 1946, 14,700,000 worked in manufacturing and only 5,595,000 in government. Today, 18,192,000 work in manufacturing and, as cited above, 18,578,000 work for government.

Government does not and cannot create wealth. It only takes from those who do. Unfortunately, when government grows too large and too intrusive, deficits and debt result.

Of the last four big tax increases—in 1982, '84, '87, and '90—none lowered the deficit and reduced spending. Not a dime from the $30 billion raised in the 1990 budget deal with Congress reduced the deficit, and there is no reason to believe that the 1993 budget, with its increased taxes, will be any more effective over the long term.

If President Clinton attacked waste and overspending in and on government, instead of zeroing in on the overstressed wallets of taxpayers, who already work more than four months of the year just to pay their tax bills, he would have bipartisan support and achieve a significant victory over deficit spending. The Government Accounting Office has identified more than $180 billion of government waste. The president ought to be talking about cutting waste, not "sacrifice," "contributions," and "investment," all euphemisms for higher taxes. If he talked about and tried to cut waste, he'd have most of the country behind him.

But the spending continues. Even adjusted for inflation, federal spending is more than 40 percent higher today than it was in 1980. (This wasn't Ronald Reagan's fault. Only Congress can appropriate money.)

Higher taxes on corporations, savers, and investors will shut off access to new capital and could destroy jobs and reduce our international competitiveness. Democrats love to tax corporations. The president initially called for a tax hike to 36 percent for companies making more than $10 million annually. But corporations, if they are to be profitable (the only reason corporations exist), must either raise prices or reduce costs by laying off workers when faced with higher taxes.

Recall the luxury boat tax that was part of the 1990 budget agreement. Fewer yachts were purchased, because higher taxes were passed along to customers in increased prices and they didn't want to pay those prices. Yacht manufacturers laid off workers and the workers applied for unemployment compensation and food stamps. The government took in less money because fewer yachts were sold.

The American Revolution began as a revolt against taxes. A new American revolution could begin over the same issue. During the Vietnam War, President Clinton's generation chanted, "Hell, no, we won't go." Those of us fed up with paying more and more of our money to government ought to refuse to give government another dime. In fact, we should be taking dimes away, forcing Big Government to go on a diet. That way government would be forced to reduce spending. There aren't enough jails to house everyone who would protest new taxes; it would only take a small percentage of us. Our slogan could be, "No way, we won't pay."

THE FOUNDING FATHERS AND TAXES

Having spent so much space criticizing the tax-and-spend policies of the Clinton administration, I think it would be useful to consider how the Founders viewed taxes, and the warnings they recorded about how government could use the power to tax to undermine freedom.

Taxes were of such concern to the Founders that they launched our revolution to do away with those they believed were unfairly and excessively imposed.

During debates over the adoption of the federal Constitution in 1787–88, those involved in the ratification process said much that we would do well to recall. Revisiting those debates in Jonathan Elliot's 1901 book, *The Debates in the Several State Conventions on the Adoption of the Federal Constitution*, is quite an education in economic philosophy.

Thomas Hartley, a colonel in the Revolutionary War and a delegate from Pennsylvania, said, "The power of taxation is then a great and important trust; but we lodge it with our own representatives, and as long as we continue virtuous we shall be safe, for they will not dare to abuse it." No one today speaks of virtue and Congress in the same breath.

The Founders wrote in Article 1, Section 8 of the Constitution that the power granted to Congress to spend money was solely to benefit the "general welfare." Thomas Jefferson explained that, far from a license to spend, the intent was to "limit the power of taxation" to matters that would provide for the welfare of "the Union." Alexander Hamilton and others concurred with Jefferson's position. So sure were they of the rightness of their beliefs that Archibald MacLaine, a patriot and spokesman from North Carolina, was moved to conclude, "Congress will not lay a single tax when it is not to the advantage of the people at large."

While the "general-welfare clause" was eventually modified by the courts, James Madison delivered a stern warning to Congress that was remarkably prescient: "If Congress can supply money indefinitely to the general welfare, and are the sole and supreme judges of the general welfare, they may take the care of religion into their own hands; they may take into their own hands the education of children, establishing in like manner schools throughout the Union; they may undertake the regulation of all roads, other than post roads.

"In short, everything from the highest object of State legislation, down to the most minute object of policy, would be thrown under the power of Congress; for every object I have mentioned would admit the application of money, and might be called, if Congress pleases, provisions for the general welfare."

That Madison was right and could see into the future has been proved in our time.

It was not cynicism, but experience, that led Massachusetts patriot John Smith to say, "It is a general maxim, that all governments find a use for as much money as they can raise. Indeed, they have commonly demands for more. . . . Congress will ever exercise their powers to levy as much money as the people can pay. They will not be restrained from direct taxes by the consideration that necessity does not require them."

Jefferson, too, saw the future of an unbridled Congress when he wrote, "We must make our election between economy and liberty or profusion and servitude. If we run into such debts as that we must be taxed in our meat and in our drink, in our necessities and our comforts, in our labors and our amusements, for our callings and our creeds, as the people of England are, our people, like them, must come to labor sixteen hours in the twenty-four, (and) give the earnings of fifteen of these to the government for their debts and daily expenses; and the sixteenth being insufficient to afford us bread, we must live, as they do now, on oatmeal and potatoes; have no time to think, no means of calling the mismanagers to account; but be glad to obtain subsistence by hiring ourselves to rivet their chains on the backs of our fellow sufferers.

"This example reads to us the salutary lesson that private fortunes are destroyed by public as well as by private extravagance. And this is the tendency of all human governments. A departure from principle in one instance becomes a precedent for a second, the second for a third, and so on, till the bulk of the society is reduced to mere automatons of misery, to have no sensibilities left, but for sinning and suffering."

Jefferson believed that the "forehorse of this frightful team is public debt. Taxation follows that, and in its train wretchedness and oppression."

Is that not the station in which this "train" has arrived? Public debt has led to higher taxes and even higher debt as Congress proves itself unable, or unwilling, to live within our means.

The American Revolution was launched because King George III went too far and it became necessary, "in the course of human events . . . for one people to dissolve the political bands which have connected them with another."

As has been said earlier, it may be time for a second American revolution.

SOCIALISM IS ALIVE AND WELL
AND COMING TO AMERICA

In defeating its archenemy of seven decades, the United States proved the superiority of its economic and political systems. Socialism was supposed to be the most compassionate and fairest monetary system on the planet. It was really nothing more than mutually shared poverty.

While most nations are abandoning socialism, the United States, incredibly, continues to flirt with it. This is like the Dallas Cowboys taking the playbook of the Buffalo Bills, a team they crushed in the 1993 Super Bowl, and using it the following season for their own team. Why would a championship football team want a playbook from the losing team? Why would a victorious nation try to adopt the economic system of a nation it has just defeated in the Cold War?

Anyone still needing a lesson in the bankruptcy of socialism should read the May 24, 1993, issue of *Forbes* magazine. In an article titled "Swedish Disease," writer Paul Klebnikov examines that country's great Socialist experiment and finds it to be on its deathbed.

Until just recently, Sweden funneled 70 percent of the country's gross domestic product into the state treasury. It then paid out 90, and in some cases 100, percent of Swedes' working incomes to the unemployed, the sick, or those who wanted to quit work and take care of their kids.

Sweden is a warning to any country that wants to follow a similar path, which is what the Clinton administration is trying to do in America. Sweden's high taxes have caused industrial production to fall 15 percent since 1989. The jobless rate was at 12 percent in mid-1993, and rising. The budget deficit accounted for a third of the central government's spending and 13 percent of the country's gross domestic product (compared to 5 percent in the U.S.). The currency was sinking faster than the dollar.

Klebnikov writes, "Sweden's welfare state has all but destroyed the country's work ethic. The absentee rate in Swedish industry reached an astounding 25 percent several years ago before recent welfare cutbacks encouraged people to work more."

What was that? Recent welfare cutbacks encouraged people to work more! Imagine if that caught on in America, as Governors Tommy Thompson of Wisconsin and John Engler of Michigan are making sure it will in their states. These governors are encouraging people to work in lieu of welfare.

Klebnikov says, "By becoming every Swede's rich grandfather, the state has destroyed most people's incentive to save." Without private savings, people become more dependent on employers and politicians.

Things are starting to change in Sweden. A new government is reducing taxes and welfare payments have been cut. A voucher system has been introduced in the public schools and capital gains taxes were reduced to 30 percent. Sweden has a long way to go, but at least it is finally moving in the right direction.

Unfortunately, except where individual initiatives are concerned, the United States isn't.

GOVERNMENT HEALTH CARE: A PRESCRIPTION FOR DISASTER

Nowhere in the United States does socialism seem as assured of obtaining a secure foothold as in the Clinton administration's health care plan, which marks the final step in the eclipse of the individual by the omnipresent and omnipotent Big Brother.

If Hillary Rodham Clinton gets her way (and she is used to it), the government will take over the nation's superb health care system. Anyone who thinks the U.S. Postal Service does a great job at a reasonable price will love the job government will try to do on the medical profession. The rest of us, which is most of the country, had better hope those TV faith healers can do some good.

Though repeatedly delayed because of President Clinton's trouble with his economic program, the health care "reform" plotted by Hillary Rodham Clinton and her band of five hundred or more secret advisers will cost a ton of money and is likely to reduce the quality of care that makes our system the best anywhere. When King Hussein of Jordan needs a checkup or surgery, he doesn't go to a hospital in Amman, he comes to the Mayo Clinic.

Congressional Budget Office Director Robert Reischauer let the cat out of the bag after assurances by Hillary Rodham Clinton that she could do the impossible: reduce costs, make health care universal, and not compromise quality.

Testifying before a House subcommittee, Reischauer said managed care, an overhaul in malpractice litigation, and less red tape will result in only modest savings. He said that covering the estimated 33.6 million uninsured (which is not a fixed number, since people move from uninsured to insured and many remain uninsured for limited periods of time) will cost an estimated $33 billion in 1994 alone. "Someone will have to pay these additional costs," he said. We know who that will be.

"If the savings from health care reform are used first to cover the uninsured," said Reischauer, "and then to reduce the high costs of private payers, not much will be left to reduce the costs of the federal programs."

Reischauer warned that "ending the tax subsidy for health insurance could also raise the number of uninsured," which means we would return to where we started, but with the quality of health care reduced for everybody.

What the administration has proposed is a form of socialized medicine that could resemble the Canadian system. Socialized medicine in Canada has created waiting lists for some surgical procedures. Many Canadian patients come to the United States for what they think is better and more accessible treatment.

Twenty-seven years after national and universal health care was adopted, Canada has started to feel the pinch. It uses tax money to pay most medical bills. It also regulates hospital budgets and doctors' fees. Yet, medical costs are rising rapidly, and for the first time patients are being required to pay extra for common medical services.

The *New York Times* catalogued Canada's health care dream. Despite efforts to control costs, revenues in the public sector are not increasing rapidly enough. While the government once paid half the cost of the health system, it now pays only 30 percent. The provinces have been forced into ever larger deficits to finance health care, which now consumes about one-third of total spending. This contributes to Canada's foreign debt because provincial bonds must be sold abroad to underwrite the deficit.

Would Americans be satisfied if government dictated which doctor they must see? Would a surgeon who receives controlled fees have the incentive to increase his knowledge and improve his skills?

There are ways, including medical IRAs, to increase coverage while maintaining quality. The direction toward socialized medicine is not one of them.

THE COPRESIDENT

If Bill Clinton is the landlord of Big Government, Hillary Rodham Clinton is the architect and builder. Hillary thinks Big Government is not only good for us, she thinks it might even be our salvation—literally.

Hillary has been a promoter of Big Government nearly all of her life. She has worked for various groups and causes, from the Legal Services Corporation to the Children's Defense Fund.

After toning down during the campaign to hide her feminist image (even wearing a headband and a mostly conservative wardrobe), the headband came off shortly after the inauguration and Hillary emerged from her hiding place to demonstrate that she wears the feminist pants in the house (and the Senate, too).

President Clinton announced that his wife would attend cabinet meetings, and she announced that meetings of her health care task force would be held in secret. Apparently the American people could not be trusted to know, until she was ready to tell us, just how she was going to "reform" health care.

President Clinton explained that the reason "copresident" Hillary Rodham Clinton would attend cabinet meetings was that "she knows more than the rest of us about a lot of things." Now, this comment was either (a) condescending, or (b) sexist, like speaking of the "little woman," followed by a knowing wink of the eye, or (c) correct . . . she really *does* know more than the cabinet and her husband, which is an incredible admission (now proving true) by a new president and a signal to the public that it was duped.

The issue has nothing to do with influence. Every president's wife does and should have that. The issue is accountability, and how the president's wife will be answerable for policies, and how we will know which came from her and which from him.

Wall Street Journal reporter Michael Frisby wrote in the December 18, 1992, edition, concerning Chief of Staff Thomas "Mack" McLarty: "There are already questions about whether Mr. McLarty is knowledgeable enough about Washington to be effective in his job—but friends suggest it may well fall to Mrs. Clinton to supply whatever savvy Mr. McLarty may be lacking."

This is frightening stuff. We don't need a "shadow president," an Imelda Marcos type who pulls policy strings and runs the government behind the scenes, with no accountability to the people. At a minimum, Hillary Rodham Clinton should be subject to the same ethics laws that apply to other staff members. Since she is creating policy, often in secret, she should have been required to testify about her views before a congressional committee. She should frequently offer herself to be questioned by the press at public news conferences, not at controlled interviews on preselected subjects by friendly interrogators.

A letter from Carole Baker of Little Rock to the editor of *Christianity Today* magazine in late 1992 was revealing. Baker wrote, "I have worked . . . to try to stop some of the programs and liberal agenda of Ms. Rodham and Mr. Clinton. Some of those programs—all attacks on the family and parental authority—were: school-based sex clinics with abortion referral [and] three-year-olds [required to go to] kindergarten . . . During Mr. Clinton's tenure as governor, we have dropped from twentieth to twenty-fifth of the twenty-eight states taking the same tests.

"I could write a book about the battles we have had to fight at the state capital because of philosophies held by the Clintons. She is far more ambitious than her husband."

That quickly became apparent in the large numbers of

administration appointments who were Hillary's friends and who were personally approved for office by her before the president nominated or appointed them.

That's too much power for an unelected and unaccountable individual.

GOVERNMENT JOBS
DON'T QUALIFY PEOPLE FOR MUCH

"Copresidents" Hillary and Bill Clinton sometimes justify increased government control of the private sector by pointing out all the jobs they're creating. But what kind of jobs are they really proposing?

When President Clinton delivered his economic message to Congress in early March 1993, he said his plan would create 500,000 jobs that year. The Senate wisely killed the measure, thanks to a Republican filibuster.

These "jobs" would have merely transferred people from one form of welfare to another, with little to show for it and no experience given to the workers that would allow them to find jobs in the private sector when the government money ran out.

A close examination of Clinton's measure by the Senate Republican Policy Committee indicated the types of jobs Clinton wanted: 50,000 people would have worked as summer employees in the Head Start program; 13,000 would work on highways; 9,000 would work on mass transit capital improvements; 14,000 would be summer school teachers; a whopping 700,000 "disadvantaged youth" would work in "summer youth employment," and 175,000 of them would work for a full year. And so it goes.

What business would hire someone who spent a summer sprucing up a government swimming pool or repairing bridges?

The economic principle that works is lowering taxes, which creates more real jobs because businesses then have more capital to invest. It worked when President Kennedy lowered taxes. It worked when Ronald Reagan cut taxes. It would have worked even better if Congress had only done its part and reduced spending. Even so, more Americans are working now than ever. Layoffs start when taxes increase and businesses cut expenses by firing workers. You don't have to be an economist to understand that business exists to make a profit and toward that end will do whatever is necessary, from raising prices to laying off workers.

Government kills business and creates economic havoc when it stifles growth with higher taxes and more regulation.

WHO OWNS THE TITLE TO
COMPASSION?

For more than three decades the debate in America has been between liberals, who favor helping the "poor" through dozens of dependency-inducing programs that keep the economy mired in record debt, and conservatives, who seek to slow the growth of these programs. Liberals howl at how insensitive conservatives are and how much they lack compassion for those less fortunate than themselves.

Notice that liberals never allow the debate to center on spending, only on tax "fairness" and paying one's "fair share." By doing this, they perpetuate the class warfare between the haves, most of whom work hard and sacrifice for what they have, and the have-nots, most of whom lack initiative, largely because government checks offer no incentive to get a job.

Liberals cornered the public-perception market on compassion when the nation lost its concept of sin and redemption and the consequences of lazy living.

Professor Marvin Olasky of the University of Texas wrote a marvelous book that traces the origin of true compassion. It's called *The Tragedy of American Compassion*. In it, Olasky notes that while most people have been relatively poor since the dawn of human history, most poor people got by because their families were intact. With the breakup of the family, the face of poverty has changed dramatically.

"Crack babies in inner-city hospitals tremble and twitch uncontrollably," Olasky writes. "Teenage mothers, alone with squalling children, fight the impulse to strike out. Women in their thirties, abandoned by husbands, wait for their number to be called in cold welfare offices. Homeless men line up impatiently at food wagons before shuffling off to eat and drink in alleys smelling of urine."

Olasky writes of the true compassion that was early America. People were expected to be their brother's and sister's keeper. Sermons regularly reminded people of their duty to care for the truly needy. But those same sermons, along with the culture, reminded people of the consequences of slothfulness and self-destructive behavior. The incentive to work and to avoid behavior that would not be in one's best interests was reinforced by the lack of welfare checks and the cultural disapproval of deviant living.

It worked. Government was there as a safety net for anyone falling through the cracks of private compassion, but it would not subsidize the lazy or those engaged in self-destructive behavior. Government was not to be a first resource, but a last resort. That thinking and that practice have been reversed in our time.

As is currently the case in Sweden, the more nonproductive Americans think they can get out of productive people, the less incentive they'll have to be productive themselves and the greater the burden to the state and the taxpayers. As government grows and produces not fewer, but more people on the dole, respect for government declines, compassion for the poor evaporates, and personal responsibility and duty to help the truly needy turns to an ugly cynicism that sees all poor people as welfare queens and undeserving louts.

That is precisely where we are in the United States in the 1990s.

In early America, what we would today call "tough love" was standard. Olasky writes, "Those who gave material aid without requiring even the smallest return were considered as much a threat to true compassion as those who turned their backs on neighbors and brothers."

Epilogue:
Promises to Keep

"Modern" is usually considered a positive word. It suggests something or someone up-to-date and "with it." Its opposite, "outmoded," suggests one who is mired in the past, still riding a horse and using a quill pen, while the rest of us celebrate the wonders of technology in our high-priced and high-speed cars and in front of our higher-speed computers.

But "modern" also has a negative side. It is a description of those who have shed the standards and truths of the past to put on the intellectual and moral clothing of the moment—which they then change frequently, like the fashions that go in and out of style on the whims of designers. This use of "modern" is most often described in intellectual and sociological circles as "modernity," and it aptly fits those in charge of moving our culture in reverse—away from the things that matter most—as we approach the new century and the beginning of the third millennium.

In a new book by E. Michael Jones called *Degenerate Moderns*, the subtitle offers a clue to the author's belief that internal moral guideposts and outward actions are connected: "Modernity as Rationalized Sexual Misbehavior."

Jones shows how some of the major leaders in modern thought and culture have rationalized their own immoral behavior and from those rationalizations spun grand theories about the way things are supposed to be.

Jones writes that in the past one hundred years, the cultural elite in the West subjected truth to desire as the final criterion of intellectual value.

In considering recent biographies of such major moderns as Freud, Kinsey, Keynes, Margaret Mead, Picasso, and others, Jones found a remarkable similarity among these people. After becoming sexually licentious early on, each invariably chose an ideology or art form that subordinated reality to the exigencies of their sexual misbehavior.

It is a fascinating and compelling argument and one for which Jones supplies heavy amounts of grist. There can be no question that those he examines—living and dead—are peddling high-octane influence in our culture of modernity.

Still, it is within the power of the individual to make up his own mind about the things that will bring true peace and happiness. While the cultural clutter is great, the things that matter most are few. Contributing to the clutter has been a blurring between what we absolutely must have—our needs—and what we would like to have—our wants. Tension, despair, depression, and personally corrupting behavior often come from lusting after things we don't really need and becoming frustrated when we don't get them, or worse, from actually getting them and finding they don't live up to their advance billing.

Because we are three-dimensional beings, each dimension—body, mind, and spirit—must be fulfilled or we sense we are incomplete. The denial of spiritual values since the sixties has produced a new yearning and longing for meaning by many of those at the front lines of that denial.

For example, television producer Norman Lear recently wrote a column for the *Washington Post* that called for a "spiritual renewal." Said Lear, "We need to make room in the culture for a public discussion of our common spiritual life in this desolate modern age. We need to discover together what is truly sacred."

Columnist Charles Krauthammer ridiculed Lear as an apostle of secularism who sees the country in the early stages of a possible spiritual renewal and wants to "get back into the game" after spending decades trying to expunge religious faith from the public square.

While Krauthammer's conclusions are valid, I think he is too harsh. Norman Lear offers permission for many to think about a dimension of their lives they have long ignored. Yes, the Boomers' drift is likely to be in the direction of New Age spiritism featuring an impersonal "god," but it's a start and it's better than what we have been getting from liberal secularists, who have succeeded in expelling God from most of public life. Some big trees began as little mustard seeds.

Shirley MacLaine is another prominent person making a plea for us to reexamine our inner selves and spiritual nature. While she believes in reincarnation and other wacky ideas, she told a convention of the American Society of Newspaper Editors in Baltimore on April 2, 1993, that newspapers should be more interested in spiritual things.

"The Founding Fathers regarded individual spirituality as an essential source of personal and social morality," MacLaine told the surprised editors. "And, from positions of leadership," she said, "they repeatedly stressed the importance of spirituality in the nation's public life. They spoke of spirituality not as the protected province of state-sanctioned pieties, but as [the province] of universe-beyond-dominion."

Never mind that MacLaine thinks she has perhaps come from a universe beyond this one and has been other people in former lives. This is a breakthrough worth pursuing.

Unfortunately, many of those who came of age in the sixties are reluctant these days to embark on a journey inward because they have lost the road map and fired the guide. So utterly did they banish God from their thinking, exchanging Him for many smaller gods who reflected their own mind-set and approved what they wished to do, that, today, they no longer know where to search for Him.

Columnist Don Feder, in his *A Jewish Conservative Looks at Pagan America*, summarizes it well: "The gods of late twentieth-century America include the doctrines of radical autonomy, of absolute rights divorced from responsibilities, of gender sameness, of self-expression which acknowledges no higher purpose, of moral relativism and sexual indulgence. Their temples are courtrooms, legislative chambers, classrooms, news rooms, and the executive suites of entertainment conglomerates and publishing firms. We are one nation under God no more."

Many are beginning to awaken to the truth that the damage we observe has been self-inflicted. Barbara Reynolds, a politically liberal columnist for *USA Today*, wrote a remarkable column for the June 25, 1993, edition of that newspaper in which she listed the now-familiar litany of symptoms of cultural breakdown.

In addressing the lawlessness and lack of social order that grips too many cities, she wrote, "Those murderous habits aren't based solely on financial poverty, but on a bankrupt human spirit caused by an absence of the spirit of God. If it weren't for the religious faithful [in cities and schools], life would be utterly hopeless.

"The downward drag started in 1963 when the court kicked prayer out of the public schools. Our moral foundation crumbled. Violent rap music, drugs, guns, and illicit sex leaped into the vacuum.

"While I don't want mandated prayers or Bible readings churning out robotic prayer warriors, you must find ways for schools and the workplace to implement values based on love, justice, and mercy, principles most religions adhere to. . . .

"My generation blew it by pushing God out of public life. Undo their mistakes. Many lives depend on it."

This is a remarkable admission, and it is true. Spending

more government money will not cure AIDS and other venereal diseases, or reduce the record numbers of abortions, or children born out of wedlock, or solve a litany of other social evils. The inner person is beyond government's reach and power.

That is why even some government leaders and other people of Barbara Reynolds's generation, such as Hillary Rodham Clinton, are beginning to explore that which they once rejected.

Mrs. Clinton's "guru" is Michael Lerner, editor of a Jewish publication called *Tikkun*. He preaches the "politics of meaning" and gives Hillary a spiritual rationale for her political programs that see government as our keeper and deliverer, even our redeemer.

As Lerner has written, the politics of meaning "addresses the psychological, ethical, and spiritual needs of Americans. It incorporates the liberal and progressive agenda, but it puts this agenda in a much deeper context."

Sounds like "designer God" to me. Still, the "politics of meaning" is a tacit admission that the Baby Boomers are beginning to realize they have missed something crucial in life. To paraphrase the Bible, which this generation worked so hard to expunge from everywhere except motel rooms, What does it profit a man or woman if he or she gains even the presidency but loses his or her own soul?

The fact is that a politics not shaped according to a proper view of Man, of God, and of history—most of which is now largely regarded as subjective, but which was once believed to be rooted in objective truth—soon becomes despotic and has no meaning except to those imposing it on the rest of us. If one is going to die and face a hereafter, and a judgment, why should the economy matter most? Other generations did not believe the economy was above all else. If they did we would have monuments and memorials to them in Washington, but there are no monuments or memorials to any president for his economic policies.

The people we remember and revere are those who believed in the things that matter most: the things of the spirit, such as honor, selflessness, humility, service to others, self-control, fidelity, and virtue. As this book has repeatedly pointed out, these qualities are not caught as one might catch a cold, ignorant of the origin of the germ. These qualities must be drummed into people and affirmed in school and the rest of culture by the state (which is charged with promoting the general welfare, not letting everybody do his own thing so as to detract from the general welfare), and in the home.

Such notions used to be so basic they were rarely discussed. They didn't have to be. They were considered "self-evident truths." That's why Thomas Jefferson saw no need to elaborate on the right to life, liberty, and the pursuit of happiness in the Declaration of Independence. He rightly believed that everyone reading what he had written in his time, which was for all time, would know precisely what he meant, because nearly everyone shared the same reasoning process, though they did not always come to identical conclusions.

On a recent visit to Philadelphia, I took the tour of Independence Hall. As I stood in the room where the Declaration of Independence was signed, the guide displayed a printed copy of the document and asked how many of us had seen the handwritten original in the National Archives. A few of us raised our hands. The guide then urged the rest to see it soon because, he said, "The ink is fading and there is nothing anyone can do about it."

What a metaphor for what ails America! The principles, values, and beliefs that once seemed indelibly written on our hearts, minds, and culture are fading and there seems to be little anyone can do to stop it.

Among those who are examining the beliefs of the generation that dropped out and began the erasure process is Wade Clark Roof, professor of religion and society at the University of California at Santa Barbara.

Roof and a team of researchers interviewed more than fifteen hundred Baby Boomers about their religious lives. They found that a disturbingly large number of them left the church and synagogue, never to return. Of those who did return, many are still on the fringes, unwilling to make a commitment (a characteristic common to this generation) to a particular faith, denomination, or creed.

Roof learned of an intense "search for spirituality" by many. He likens the typical "seeker," however, to a person who browses through a supermarket but never buys or eats the food and, thus, slowly starves to death.

Roof credits evangelical and conservative churches with giving the Boomers not what they want (at least not initially), but what they need: ". . . the evangelicals, with their more clear-cut beliefs and boundaries, are better equipped to provide [spiritual nourishment] than are the liberals."

Boundaries, rules, order, conviction, certainty, purpose, meaning—all of these the Boomers overthrew in their relentless pursuit of social anarchy, believing it would usher in an Aquarian Age and that they were uniquely equipped to bring peace on earth and goodwill to men, history's lessons to the contrary.

Especially during the past thirty years, the West has operated on the Enlightenment principle that Man is autonomous and perfectible. Surely there is sufficient evidence to discredit this view, except perhaps in the minds of those who choose not to be persuaded. As John Gray wrote in his review of John Rawls's book *Political Liberalism* in the *New York Times Book Review*, "Mr. Rawls's abandonment of liberalism as a worldview reflects the collapse of confidence in secular humanism in our time. Aside from a handful of fundamentalist liberals like Francis Fukuyama, the author of *The End of History and the Last Man*, there can be few who any longer take seriously the Enlightenment expectation of progress toward a universal rationalist civilization."

Maybe, but those who once did will not relinquish power and position until they have adopted another worldview that suits them at least as well.

The good news is that we still retain ultimate power over the shape and direction of our lives and those of our children. We don't have to be victims of either tyranny by government or moral tyranny by a pagan culture.

Former First Lady Barbara Bush offered sound counsel for those who would heed it at the 1990 Wellesley College commencement.

Some of the budding feminists at the women's school sought to disinvite Mrs. Bush from speaking. They considered her a poor role model because, they said, her fame was derived from the man she married. When she said she would bring Raisa Gorbachev with her, the protesting students relented, saying that Raisa was a woman they could admire.

Mrs. Bush refused to flinch over this insult and went anyway, delivering a message that was so rooted in common sense and historical evidence that just two generations ago it would have seemed unnecessary.

She told the graduates that they must not indulge in self, but must "believe in something larger than yourself." She said that first and foremost, "life must really have joy."

She married George Bush, she said, because "he made me laugh." Imagine. She didn't even ask for a prenuptial agreement on how the housework would be divided.

Then she delivered this powerful punch: "But as important as your obligations as a doctor, a lawyer, a business leader will be, you are a human being first, and those human connections with spouses, with children, with friends are the most important investment you will ever make.

"At the end of your life," she said, "you will never regret not having passed one more test, winning one more verdict, or not closing one more deal. You will regret time not spent with a husband, a child, a friend, or a parent."

As if this weren't enough to set feminist teeth grinding, Mrs. Bush then delivered the coup de grace: ". . . whatever the era, whatever the times, one thing will never change: Fathers and mothers, if you have children, they must come first. . . . Your success as a family, our success as a society, depends not on what happens in the White House, but on what happens in your house."

Above all else, these are the things that matter most: faith in a personal God who is knowable, family, freedom to pursue one's dreams, and keeping most of the gain one gets through hard and honest work.

In discarding the first of that list, faith in God, the Baby Boomers also lost the concept of sin, which teaches that Man is not basically good, but is flawed from within and can never be made perfect from without. This loss is crucial, as theologian Michael Novak, writing in the April 1993 issue of the Catholic magazine *Crisis*, points out:

"One cannot understand America and certainly not its founders or institutions, if one does not understand the Jewish and Christian consciousness of the reality of sin. Without that understanding, one is living in a fool's paradise. Without that, the institutions will not function or long endure. This republic was designed for sinners.

"There is no use trying to build a republic for saints. There are too few of them, and even the ones there are, are difficult to live with. No, if you wish to build a republic that will last, you must design it for sinners. That is the only 'moral majority' there is . . . a republic of sinners—and, therefore, a republic with checks and balances, as well as other 'auxiliary precautions' (to employ the phrase of James Madison, well-taught as he was by Christian teachers).

"Biblical realism commands us to keep a taut rein upon utopian instincts, and spontaneously to be distrustful of 'utopic theorists' (as the Federalist again insists)."

Novak writes that the republic was not founded to

redeem us. Its purposes were much more limited: ". . . many public policies of recent generations were established as if human beings were not sinners, as if sin did not exist, and as if government could save us and make us happy and all right. That is exactly why government has fallen into disrepute. Government is not our savior. No city of man is the City of God. The massive illusion that citizens are inherently and infallibly good, and that government officials may establish happiness on earth, has met reality. Entire realms of social and psychological theory, based upon utopic theories, have failed to account for the ordinary sinfulness of ordinary human beings. Look around you. You see the ruins."

Novak concludes on an upbeat note: "Biblical realism will rise again. It always has."

We do not have to be the victims of culture, of government, or of circumstances. The greatest power on earth is not what outsiders do to us, but what we do to ourselves. Government cannot control the sexual behavior of a teenager, or force a man to be a real father to his children, or to covet integrity, honesty, and virtue. But people can decide to do these things for themselves, to be the masters of their circumstances, not its victims.

We don't need to be looking for new leaders so much as we need to *be* new leaders. There is no greater influence on our lives than that which we ourselves bring to our lives and those closest to us. We can be an influence for evil, or an influence for good. It is our choice, and we have to select between those short-term, seemingly pleasurable experiences that promise everything but have brought near ruin to our nation, and the things that matter most.

Evangelist Billy Graham has observed that America is not at a crossroads, as some say, but rather a long way down the wrong road, and that it needs to come back to the crossroads and take the right road. America is more than a country, more than geographically defined states, counties, and cities.

America is people who once shared a common idea, a set of values and principles that defined a nation more than fruited plains and purple mountains' majesty.

So, Americans are a long way down the wrong road. While government has a role in securing certain rights and controlling certain behavior, it cannot kidnap us and force us all to take the ride in the right direction. It takes millions of individual decisions to strike out in a different direction.

At a White House ecumenical prayer breakfast in September 1993, President Clinton correctly noted that government "can't possibly do anything for anybody in this country unless they're willing to do something for themselves . . . you cannot change somebody's life from the outside in unless there is also some change from the inside out."

But then the president added, incorrectly I think, that government can create the "common good" in America and that he would try hard "to create a new sense of common purpose." Government is incapable of doing such a thing. Only people who hold similar values can do that.

The journey of a thousand miles begins with a single step. The redemption of a great nation can begin with a single and powerful decision by one "ordinary" person that influences others to make similar decisions because they perceive how right and beautiful and good that decision is.

The hour may be late, but the choices remain for each of us, and the benefits to those who choose wisely will affect not only they themselves, but generations to come.

The broken promises of the past were not—indeed, they could not have been—kept. The promises for the future, rooted in a new birth of spiritual, political, and economic freedom, can and must be kept. We owe it to those who have gone before. If we fail, we will be held accountable by those who are yet to come.